DATE DUE

Canadian Fiction Studies

Other volumes in preparation

Introducing

HUGH MACLENNAN'S

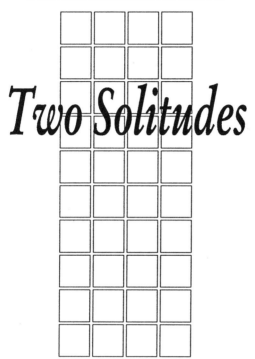

Two Solitudes

A READER'S GUIDE BY

Linda Leith

E C W   P R E S S

Copyright © ECW PRESS, 1990

CANADIAN CATALOGUING IN PUBLICATION DATA

Leith, Linda.
Introducing Hugh MacLennan's Two Solitudes

(Canadian fiction studies ; no. 10)
Bibliography : p. 85.
Includes index.
ISBN 1–55022–018–7

I. MacLennan, Hugh, 1907–   . Two Solitudes.
I. Title. II. Series.

PS8525.L45T875 1990   C813'.54   C89-095004-0
PR9199.3.M334T875 1990

This book has been published with the assistance of grants
from The Canada Council, the Ontario Arts Council, and
the Government of Canada Department of Communications.

The cover features a reproduction of the dust-wrapper
from the first edition of *Two Solitudes*, courtesy of the
Thomas Fisher Rare Book Library, University of Toronto.
Frontispiece photograph from the *Montreal Star*, photographer
unknown, courtesy National Archives of Canada [PA-169904].
Design and imaging by ECW Type & Art, Oakville, Ontario.
Printed by University of Toronto Press, North York, Ontario.

Distributed by Butterworths Canada Ltd.
75 Clegg Road, Markham, Ontario L6G 1A1

Published by ECW PRESS,
307 Coxwell Avenue, Toronto, Ontario M4L 3B5

Table of Contents

☐ A Note on the Author ☐

Linda Leith, who was educated at McGill University and at the University of London, England, has taught English for fourteen years at John Abbott College in Ste-Anne-de-Bellevue, Quebec, and has written articles on Canadian literature and on science fiction. She has recently edited *Telling Differences: New English Fiction from Quebec* (Montreal: Véhicule), she is the publisher and editor of *Matrix* magazine, and she is preparing a booklength study of English Quebec fiction since 1945.

REFERENCES AND ACKNOWLEDGEMENTS

Parenthetical page references throughout this monograph are to the standard 1986 Macmillan edition of *Two Solitudes*. The only significantly different edition of the novel is the school edition published by Macmillan in 1951 and "arranged" by Claude T. Bissell. This considerably abridged version ends with the death of Athanase Tallard in Chapter 29 and therefore excludes the concluding chapter of Part II as well as the whole of Parts III and IV.

I am grateful to Robert Lecker of McGill University, at whose suggestion this monograph was written. In writing it I have benefitted considerably from Elspeth Cameron's biographical and bibliographical work on Hugh Mac-Lennan. I conducted the interview with MacLennan referred to in this study on 6 February 1987; I interviewed Mavis Gallant on 12 May 1987. I would like to thank both these writers for their assistance. Elizabeth McIninch cast a historian's eye over the notion of national unity prevalent in English Canada during the 1940s. Andrew Rodger of the National Archives of Canada was helpful in finding photographs of MacLennan.

Finally I wish gratefully to acknowledge the generous support of the FCAR (Fonds pour la Formation des Chercheurs et l'aide à la Recherche) in Quebec; of the Social Sciences and Humanities Research Council in Ottawa; and of the Research and Development Committee of John Abbott College.

Introducing
Hugh MacLennan's
Two Solitudes

Chronology

1907   20 March, John Hugh MacLennan born in Glace Bay, Nova Scotia to Dr. Samuel MacLennan and Katherine MacQuarrie.

1914–18   World War I.

1915   The MacLennans move to Halifax, Nova Scotia, where Hugh attends Tower Road School.

1915–16   Dr. MacLennan serves overseas with the Dalhousie Medical Unit.

1917   In the spring, the MacLennans move into the house at 197 South Park Street, Halifax which will be Hugh's home until he leaves for Oxford. On 6 December the *Imo* and the French munitions ship the *Mont Blanc* collide in Halifax harbour, causing the greatest man-made explosion in human history before the atomic bomb. Some 2000 people are killed, 9000 are injured, and over 200 survivors are permanently blinded.

1918   Hugh, aged 12, moves into a tent in the back yard of the MacLennan family house. He sleeps in this tent winter and summer until his departure for Oxford in 1928.

1921   William Lyon Mackenzie King is first elected Prime Minister of Canada.

1924   MacLennan graduates from Halifax County Academy with the Yeoman prize in Latin and Greek.

1924–28   Dalhousie University, B.A. Honours in Latin and Greek.

1928   In his graduating year, awarded Governor-General's Gold Medal for Classics and the Rhodes Scholarship for Canada-at-Large; in October he enrolls in Honours Moderations and Literae Humaniores (Greats) and takes up residence at Oriel College, Oxford.

1929	The Great Depression begins with the Stock Market crash; at home for the summer, MacLennan becomes Maritimes singles tennis champion.
1930	University singles tennis champion (Oxford).
1931	The Statute of Westminster; Canada becomes a sovereign state.
1928–32	During his years at Oxford MacLennan travels widely in Europe and begins writing poetry; in 1931 a book of his poetry is rejected by three London publishers.
1932	Oxford B.A. Third Class in Literae Humaniores; as is usual, MacLennan accordingly also acquires an M.A. from Oxford.
1932	[June] Sails from Southampton on the ss *Pennland*, where he meets and falls in love with Dorothy Duncan.
1932	[Summer] MacLennan applies for a teaching position to each university with a Classics Department in Canada. Only two universities have openings, and MacLennan is turned down in favour of Englishmen.
1932	[October] Enters Princeton University where he is awarded the John Harding Page Fellowship of $400; alienated from his doctoral studies, he devotes much of his time to writing fiction and exploring socialist ideas.
1933	MacLennan and Dorothy Duncan get engaged; Adolf Hitler becomes Chancellor of Germany.
1934	MacLennan's first novel, "So All Their Praises," is accepted for publication in New York, but the publisher goes out of business before the book can be published.
1935	Ph.D. Princeton and publication of *Oxyrhynchus: An Economic and Social Study*; in October MacLennan accepts a teaching job at Lower Canada College in Montreal.
1936	Marries Dorothy Duncan in Wilmette, Illinois, 22 June; Maurice Duplessis is first elected Premier of Quebec at the head of the Union Nationale party.
1936–39	Spanish Civil War.
1937	Hugh and Dorothy meet Marian and Frank R. Scott and are introduced to the Co-operative Commonwealth

Federation (forerunner of the New Democratic Party); MacLennan joins no party; during the summer he visits the Soviet Union and Scandinavia; he reacts negatively to the Soviet system and favours Scandinavian-style democratic socialism.

1938   Attempts to publish second novel, "A Man Should Rejoice." Duell, Sloan and Pearce in New York express interest in the manuscript; it is never published. Reads Ringuet's *Trente Arpents*.

1938   Kristallnacht: Nazi pogrom against the Jews all over Germany.

1939   Death of Dr. Samuel MacLennan.

1939–45 World War II.

1941   *Barometer Rising* is published.

1942   Hugh and Dorothy first rent a house in North Hatley in the Eastern Townships of Quebec, where they will spend every summer.

1945   *Two Solitudes* is published and becomes a bestseller in the United States and Canada; MacLennan resigns from Lower Canada College to devote himself to writing fulltime; Hugh and Dorothy buy a house in North Hatley, "Stone Hedge"; the war in Europe ends.

1945   6 August, an atomic bomb is dropped on Hiroshima; three days later another is dropped on Nagasaki; Japan surrenders August 14.

1946   Governor-General's Award for Fiction for *Two Solitudes*. Dorothy wins the Governor-General's Award for Non-Fiction for her book *Partner in Three Worlds*.

1947–48 Dorothy's health declines dramatically.

1948   *The Precipice* is published.

1949   Second Governor-General's Award for *The Precipice*; publication of *Cross-Country* (essays) prompted by the need to pay mounting medical expenses for Dorothy.

1950   Third Governor-General's Award for *Cross-Country*.

1950–53 Korean War.

1951	*Each Man's Son* is published; MacLennan works as a consultant for the National Film Board; joins the English Department of McGill University as a part-time lecturer in September.
1952	Fellow of the Royal Society of Canada.
1954	*Thirty and Three*, a collection of MacLennan's essays edited by Dorothy Duncan, is published.
1955	Fourth Governor-General's Award for *Thirty and Three*.
1957	Dorothy Duncan dies April 22.
1959	*The Watch that Ends the Night* is published; MacLennan marries Frances Aline Walker ("Tota") in Montreal, 15 May; death of Maurice Duplessis, Premier of Quebec.
1960	Fifth Governor-General's Award for *The Watch that Ends the Night*; Election of the Liberal Party of Quebec under Jean Lesage: the Quiet Revolution begins.
1960–62	Three collections of essays are published: *Scotchman's Return and Other Essays*, *McGill: The Story of a University*, and *Seven Rivers of Canada*.
1963	FLQ bombings in Montreal; November 22 the assassination of President Kennedy in Dallas, Texas; *Deux Solitudes* appears in French translation for the first time in Paris.
1964	Appointed to a full-time position in the English Department at McGill.
1967	Canada's Centennial year; Expo 67 in Montreal; *Return of the Sphinx* is published.
1968	Becomes full professor of English, McGill University; Pierre Elliott Trudeau is elected Prime Minister of Canada.
1970	FLQ kidnappings and declaration of the War Measures Act.
1976	The Parti Québécois led by René Lévesque is elected to the government of Quebec.
1979	Professor emeritus at McGill.
1980	Referendum on Sovereignty-Association for Quebec in May; in August MacLennan's last novel, *Voices in Time*, is published.

The Importance of the Work

Two Solitudes is no ordinary novel. One of a handful of Canadian novels of the 1940s that mark the beginnings of contemporary Canadian fiction, it is in addition uniquely important in its attempt to come to terms with the strained relations between the French and English of Canada and to find a form that can accommodate the duality of Canadian experience. There can be no surprise when so ambitious a project falls short of success, as MacLennan's certainly does. Like Icarus, MacLennan is trying for the sun when his wings fail him. We may think him foolish and wrong-headed, we may know him doomed, but we have to marvel at his daring.

MacLennan's situation as a Canadian writer in the 1940s is very like that of his protagonist Paul Tallard who, in the second half of *Two Solitudes*, discovers his own vocation as a novelist. Paul knows that writing about Canada will present special problems because his readers will be ignorant of the essential Canadian clashes and values. As Canada is "a country that no one knew," a writer has to create background "from scratch" if his story is to become intelligible. "He could afford to take nothing for granted. He would have to build the stage and props for his play, and then write the play itself" (364–65).

Returning home from visiting his brother Marius, a French-Canadian nationalist, Paul finds himself able to draft the design of a full novel. "Its material and symbols lay ready in his subconscious: the dilemma that had nearly strangled him all his life and which at last he had managed to escape." The theme of his book begins to emerge "out of Marius, out of his own life, out of the feeling he had in his bones for his own province and the others surrounding it" (375–76). *Two Solitudes* ends with Paul going off to war without having

13

finished his own novel of Canada. The book that he has been drafting, though, and the dilemma that he can now finally view "as though it belonged to another person," are those that we have become familiar with in our own reading of *Two Solitudes*. Paul's novel, in effect, is the one we are reading.

MacLennan's attempt in *Two Solitudes* is no less than to make Canada known to the world, to create Canada. His unapologetic focus on Canadian settings and issues was new in the 1940s, and its importance should not be underestimated. Writers play a largely unacknowledged role in their articulation of issues of social import and simply in naming places and problems — in applying words to the situation that people find themselves in at a specific time and in a specific place. This is most pressing, and it is also most difficult, in the case of a new literature shaking off colonial influences. It is what American writers like James Fenimore Cooper and Nathaniel Hawthorne were doing in the mid-nineteenth century. It is what MacLennan does in *Barometer Rising* in 1941 and then in *Two Solitudes* in 1945.

Probably the best measure of a novel's importance is the effect it has had on other writers, and *Two Solitudes* has had a massive impact on the course of Canadian writing. Mavis Gallant was living in Montreal during the 1940s, writing voluminously, and working as a journalist. In a 1987 interview that I conducted with her she said: "The novels that made the great impression on people were *Two Solitudes* — that was enormous — and [Gwethalyn Graham's] *Earth and High Heaven*."

Gallant knows her French-Canadian characters intimately — there is no comparison between her and MacLennan here — and her fictional accounts of French-English relations in "Bernadette" and in her Linnet Muir stories especially are far more sophisticated than MacLennan's, but they could not have been written as she wrote them if she had never read *Two Solitudes*. This is clearest when her imagery echoes MacLennan's, as when she describes isolated groups in Montreal society as "schools of tropical fish" (this is in "The Doctor"). MacLennan himself had not only vividly described "sharks and barracuda" in the tropics (68–69), but had also, in a related image, viewed Canadian society as consisting of "little puddles with big fish in each one of them" (30). MacLennan's influence can be traced even when the lines of descent are not so clear as they

are in this instance. Unlike Paul and unlike MacLennan, Gallant —
all subsequent chroniclers of Canadian society — have found the
stage and props already in place, and have accordingly been free to
focus on the play itself.

The novel's long-standing impact may be judged in part by a letter
that Margaret Laurence wrote to MacLennan in 1970: "I feel very
deeply that I owe you a debt of gratitude as a novelist. It was really
only through your novels, and those of Ethel Wilson, and Sinclair
Ross, and very few others, that I came to an understanding of the
simple fact that novels could be written here, out of one's own
background, and that in fact this was the only true soil for me to write
out of" (Calgary archive 3.3.44).

The impact of *Two Solitudes* has been so considerable that it is
hardly surprising to find it has invited some of its successors to rebel
against it. Once a pioneering writer has compellingly provided us
with a sense of ourselves, a reaction sets in as younger writers go out
of their way to distance themselves from him. Henry James so
distanced himself from Hawthorne. And since the late 1960s — 1967
was the nadir of MacLennan's career as Canadian critics over-
whelmingly rejected the idea of Canada articulated in *Return of the
Sphinx* — some younger writers have distanced themselves from
MacLennan. The narrator in Scott Symons's iconoclastic novel, *Place
d'Armes*, which appeared in 1967, says, "Yes — everything I am doing
disproves the *Two Solitudes* . . . but that's only incidental." And in
1988 John Metcalf can write that "literary nationalism has boosted
and bloated the reputations" of many Canadian writers including
Hugh MacLennan whose books are "in the main, dull and flawed.
They were old-fashioned when they were written and are now
antiquated" (31).

This reaction is another vital stage in the development of the
literature. Important as it is for a MacLennan to provide us with a
sense of ourselves, it is equally important that we then move on —
that we explore more exciting aesthetic possibilities and that we open
ourselves up to a broader world. The critic's job here is to appreciate
not only the accomplishments of the newer writers but the extent to
which this accomplishment is made possible by the work of a Mac-
Lennan. Critic Peter Buitenhuis responds to Symons's remark with,
"Of course! But *Two Solitudes* was *there*; it constituted a creative act
that defined the situation and is now a feature of the landscape of

Montreal. In subject matter then, if not in technique, MacLennan has been the great trail-blazer; he has journeyed alone into unknown territory of the Canadian mind" (19).

Younger writers may enjoy kicking a MacLennan in the teeth. Our job as critics is to understand that the reason they can do this with such gleeful confidence is that they are standing on his shoulders. The novel does of course have its faults. No one really doubts the importance of *Two Solitudes* as a Canadian social and historical document, but describing a work of fiction as "important" in its "subject matter" is to damn it with faint praise. MacLennan himself makes no great claims for the literary merit of *Two Solitudes*,[1] and others have not hesitated to ask pointed questions about whether it works *as a novel*. Has it been overpraised simply because of what it has to say about Canada? Is there not a paradox in the fact that a novel considered important for breaking new ground in Canadian literature is considered to be formally traditional and even archaic? These are questions that demand an answer.

Critics today are less wildly enthusiastic than they were about the novel in 1945, but they tend to view the novel as important and as limited in the same ways and for the same reasons as they always have. The strengths and the weaknesses of *Two Solitudes* are not somehow universal and immutable, though; they are mostly the strengths and weakness of its time. In the interim the Quiet Revolution changed Quebec forever, the Church faded into the background, capital moved from the bastions of English Montreal to Toronto and beyond, and we have seen terrorist kidnappings, a democratic *indépendantiste* government in Quebec, a Referendum, and most recently the Meech Lake Accord under which Quebec is viewed as "within Canada a distinct society." We go back to *Two Solitudes* now not only because it is always interesting to see for ourselves what the fuss is about and to form our own judgement on a classic. We also go back to it to see how MacLennan struggled with the formal difficulties inherent in writing what he boldly calls "a novel of Canada." In some important ways he failed to resolve those difficulties. In some ways he succeeded more than has hitherto been appreciated. Much of his novel's lasting importance in Canadian literature will be that it can give us a measure of how much times and standards of judgement have changed. *Two Solitudes* allows us to see where we came from, in literary as well as in historical terms.

Critical Reception

Two Solitudes, one of the most popular Canadian novels ever written, was first published in New York on January 17, 1945. The entire first printing of 4500 copies had sold out by noon of that day, by which time several rave reviews of the novel had already appeared. One of these was in the extremely influential *New York Times*, where Orville Prescott described Hugh MacLennan as a "creative artist using the novel as a medium for the novel's best and fundamental purpose — the telling of a story about people whose concerns are made emotionally important, whose affairs can illuminate a general situation." *Two Solitudes*, Prescott concluded, "is superbly vital." A few days later the Canadian poet Leo Kennedy hailed *Two Solitudes* in the *Chicago Sun Book Week* as "the GREAT Canadian Novel." No less extravagant praise was lavished on the novel in many Canadian publications. *The Gazette* [Montreal] reviewer described it as "the outstanding Canadian novel of this or any other year," and William Deacon said in *The Globe and Mail* [Toronto], "Considering style, theme, characters, craftsmanship, significance and integrity, *Two Solitudes* may well be considered the best and most important Canadian novel ever published."

Loud as the chorus of praise undoubtedly was, though, there were dissident voices raised right from the start. Diana Trilling, writing in *The Nation* in February 1945, says the novel is "pedagogically inspired," it has very little true drama, and it lacks skill in narrative, characterization, and style. *Two Solitudes*, she writes, represents "one of those rare instances in which an author's seriousness and decency do a very good job as proxy for art." And the *Queen's Quarterly* reviewer — "I.M.S." — finds the novel "disappointing" because "the author is too aloof from the characters. Their problems are an academic study." This review is also scathing about several "glaring and irritating absurdities," about MacLennan's lack of humour, and about his account of Paul and Heather's first embrace: if this scene "satisfies the author's artistic criterion, his failure to write a great novel needs no further explanation."

Nearly half a century has passed since *Two Solitudes* was published. Since that time Canada and Quebec — the societies which are MacLennan's principal subject — have changed almost out of recognition. The nationalism of the 1940s that fuelled some of the praise MacLennan received in Canada when his novel appeared was centred on hopes for national unity. Since the 1960s that has slowly made way instead for a more dualistic vision and a recognition of the distinctiveness of Quebec. Over the same period the Canadian literary culture to which MacLennan's novel contributed mightily has developed to a degree and a sophistication unimaginable in 1945. When we evaluate *Two Solitudes* today, we view it through glasses coloured by the long list of Canadian fiction writers who have influenced us in the interim and helped refine our literary sensibilities. In the wake of such writers as Leonard Cohen, Mordecai Richler, Margaret Laurence, Alice Munro, Timothy Findley, Mavis Gallant, Margaret Atwood, and Michael Ondaatje — to mention only these — probably no one today would agree with Leo Kennedy's ebullient assessment of *Two Solitudes*; probably no one would describe it as an unqualified success.

Though we look on it more coolly today, opinions of the novel have in other ways remained surprisingly unchanged since 1945. *Two Solitudes* assumed almost immediately the status of a Canadian literary institution, and this status remains quite untouched even today. It had already sold some 700,000 copies worldwide by about 1967 (the most recent date for which a global figure is available), and today it continues very respectably to sell some 5000 copies annually in Canada.[2] Assailed though it has always been by commentators more or less severely critical of its qualities as a work of fiction, *Two Solitudes* has proved to be a tough literary nut.

The volume of critical commentary on his work would suggest that MacLennan has been thoroughly discussed. Five booklength studies of his work appeared in close succession between 1969 and 1973, as did a sixth study, by Patricia Morley, focussed on MacLennan and Leonard Cohen. This has been followed by Elspeth Cameron's substantial biographical and bibliographical work, by a special issue of *The Journal of Canadian Studies* devoted to MacLennan, and by a 1983 Twayne study. As most of his major critics are, in addition, in substantial agreement about MacLennan's work, critical opinion has apparently concluded there is not much more to say about him. In her recent study of Maritime fiction, Janice Kulyk Keefer notes without enthusiasm that "MacLennan's vision of Canada, as elaborated in *Two Solitudes* and *Return of the Sphinx*, has become part of our general cultural history" (214), and she sums up by observing that "The question of MacLennan's status and stature in the field of Canadian letters should long have ceased to be a burning one" (213).

The most striking feature of the novel's critical reception is neither the exuberance with which it has been praised, nor the severity with which it has been damned. Given how dramatically the world around the novel has indeed changed since 1945, what is most remarkable is that *Two Solitudes* has been praised and damned for effectively the same reasons and in effectively the same ways for nearly 50 years.

From the very beginning critical opinion admired what MacLennan had to say in this "novel of Canada" while expressing more or less serious reservations about how he said it. The critical consensus is that MacLennan's novel is important but didactic. The importance is associated with MacLennan's exploration of the Canadian identity in the novel generally, and specifically with the marriage between Paul Tallard and Heather Methuen, which is typically interpreted as representing a "marriage" of the French and English of Canada. The didacticism for which MacLennan is more or less severely criticized is associated with his failings as a stylist.

Even some of the most extravagant of the early newspapers reviews tended to praise the importance of MacLennan's accomplishment for Canada rather than focus on any of the formal qualities of his writing. In a glowing review in *The Canadian Forum*, for example, Eleanor McNaught said of the novel that "here is the substance of Canada, her countryside, her cities, her conflicting cultures, and, above all, her people." The focus on MacLennan's contribution to Canada's development as a nation was indeed so widespread that the novel, quite unusually for a work of fiction, attracted the lively interest of historians. Arthur R.M. Lower's *Colony to Nation*, which traced French- and English-Canadian history, would break new ground on its appearance in 1946. In a review published in *Canadian Historical*

Review Lower claims that MacLennan's novel is a milestone passed in Canada (328). Merrill Denison, who was to write the history of some of Canada's major industries, comments in his review in *Saturday Review of Literature* that the subject of the novel is "at the very core of Canada's future" and concludes that "*Two Solitudes* tells a first-rate story in an accomplished and adult manner and, perhaps more importantly at the present time, presents a sincere and unprejudiced picture of Canada's great internal conflict" (Goetsch 104). And Mason Wade, whose history of French Canada would be published ten years later, wrote that the novel is "required reading for every Canadian who is concerned with the fundamental problem of his national life."

THE CRITICAL CONSENSUS IN ENGLISH CANADA

This view of the fundamental moral worthiness *Two Solitudes* can be followed through most critical work on the novel that has appeared in the intervening years. This work is mostly accomplished, and though Buitenhuis and Lucas are the most consistently perceptive and stimulating in their brief monographs, they are not the only critics with valuable personal insights into MacLennan's work generally and *Two Solitudes* particularly. Diverse as these insights are, however, MacLennan criticism shows a remarkable degree of agreement on questions of central importance to our understanding of his novels. Indeed it is virtually unanimous in its reading of MacLennan's sympathies for French Canada, for example; in its admiration for Athanase Tallard; and in its view that the marriage of Paul Tallard and Heather Methuen symbolizes the union of French and English Canada. As it is impractical here to quote what the critics have had to say on all these questions, let this last issue provide our example of critical consensus.

George Woodcock writes that the marriage of Paul and Heather "symbolizes a course which MacLennan hopes the peoples of Canada can follow, freeing themselves from old prejudices and hatreds, and coming together in the marriage of two solitudes" (1969, 77). Alec Lucas considers the marriage "suggests a reconciliation of two solitudes" (20), and Hugo McPherson describes it as "a French-English marriage" (212). D.O. Spettigue concurs that it is "a symbolic marriage of the two founding peoples" (491). Warren Stevenson refers to "the fact that Paul is of French and Heather of English extraction" (59); W.J. Keith writes about "the marriage of French-Canadian Paul and English-Canadian Heather"(1985, 135); T.D. Mac-Lulich discusses how their marriage is "meant to point to a reconciliation of French and English" (49); and Keefer refers to this as a marriage of "different national types," "Canadien and Quebecker" (215).

Most of these commentators are unanimous, too, in considering the marriage provides rather too neat a conclusion to MacLennan's plot and that he seems to be forcing a meaning on to his story (MacLulich 49). Some even suggest, though only *en passant*, that MacLennan may be lacking in political acumen (Keith 1985, 135). Peter Buitenhuis is the only one of the major critics, however, to have remarked that Paul is not at all typical of French Canada. Buitenhuis nonetheless agrees with the other critics that the marriage is "the symbolic union of the two cultures," that "the French-Canadian characters are on the whole portrayed sympathetically," and that Athanase Tallard is "perhaps the most appealing character that Mac-Lennan has yet drawn" (36, 39).

As well as agreeing about the worthiness of MacLennan's message, the critics are also generally agreed that he is a didactic writer. Woodcock treats a great deal of Canadian literature dismissively when he argues that MacLennan's didacticism "would appear irredeemable old-fashioned" in "more sophisticated literary traditions" (1969, 48). Lucas, one of MacLennan's most sympathetic readers, sees him as "essentially a religious novelist" and describes his novels as "parables centred on religious humanism" (57). W.J. Keith, in *Canadian Literature in English*, argues that MacLennan "is a didactic novelist, a teacher or nothing, and his didacticism has an unabashedly nationalistic flavour" (134). In MacLennan's novels, Keith further concurs with his predecessors, "content takes precedence over artistry": MacLennan's "matter" in *Two Solitudes* has always seemed to the critics "more important than his manner" (1983, 575).

All kinds of individual nuances and interests aside, the consensus is: MacLennan is saying something both worthy and important; what a pity that he did not say it with more flair. The most frequently cited flaws in MacLennan's writing are the relative weakness of Parts III and IV of the novel and the characterization of Paul Tallard. Already in 1969 Buitenhuis could with justification note that "Most critics have united in thinking that the first part of the novel, up to the death of Athanase Tallard, is the best writing MacLennan has done. The second part tends towards . . . generalization and abstraction" (30). The novel never quite recovers, the argument goes, after Athanase Tallard's death because Paul, whose development is the focus of attention in the rest of the novel, is no match for this strong and vividly realized character. An extreme instance of this view is Claude Bissell's 1951 schools edition of the novel, which simply concludes with Athanase's death, lopping chapters 30–53 off altogether. His justification for this abridgement of the novel is that the concluding sections, while "not without interest," "cannot avoid giving the impression of an extended afterthought," and he argues that his edition "is not a truncated version, but a work of art complete in itself" ("Introduction," xxii-xxiii).

There have always been a few critics whose views differ substantially from the mainstream view: Cameron mentions the points of view of Marxist, Catholic, and some French-Canadian commentators who reviewed the novel in 1945. While such points of view have not often been heard in the intervening years — they are not well represented in academic English-Canadian literary circles — they have not entirely faded from the scene. In his polemical *Canadian Literature: Surrender or Revolution*, Robin Mathews flies in the face of the critical consensus when he commends MacLennan's nationalism while deploring his conservatism. A more recent, and a better argued, alternative approach is taken by Gary Boire in an essay criticizing the stance various modernist Canadian writers take towards history. Boire attacks *Two Solitudes* for perpetuating the ideological values of the majority culture and for effectively excluding the indigenous populations from his vision of Canada.

In English-Canadian literary criticism, however, the few exceptions help prove the critical rule. All in all MacLennan gets an "A," as it were, for content; and anything (depending on the critic) ranging from a "C" to an "F" for form.

Literary critics rarely distinguish quite so baldly between admirable "content" and ineffective "form": are form and content not supposed to be inextricably connected? It is furthermore not at all clear whether these critics have really thought their view of *Two Solitudes* through. It is a view that has disastrous implications. If the novel fails as a work of fiction, is it not then a document of purely historical interest? Why should we consider it a classic? What good reason can these critics suggest for reading the novel today?

It is clear that *Two Solitudes* has been central to the development of English-Canadian literature, just as it is clear to almost all commentators that MacLennan is in many ways old-fashioned, heavy-handed, and in some respects (especially in his handling of love scenes) an embarrassingly poor novelist.

Rather than resorting to the finally disastrous distinction between content and form, however, the critic might look back at the novel itself. For a careful re-reading of *Two Solitudes* reveals not that MacLennan's "matter," as Keith argues, "is invariably more important than his manner" (1983, 575) but that, on the contrary, MacLennan's style is both important in its own right and is inextricably linked with the substance of what he has to say. A re-reading of *Two Solitudes* further reveals that in Parts III and IV of the novel MacLennan is for the most part writing the same way and using the same techniques of characterization as in Parts I and II — and that the flaws in these later sections are the result not of the "weakness" of Paul compared to Athanase so much as of the change in narrative genre. A re-reading reveals, too, that the marriage of Paul and Heather cannot be viewed as a marriage between the French and English of Canada. Though MacLennan's vision of Canada — and his particular failings as a novelist — have been quite taken for granted, a re-reading raises new and perhaps even burning questions about its place in what Keefer terms "our general cultural history" (214).

THE NOVEL'S RECEPTION IN FRENCH CANADA

In French Canada the novel has had a slight reception, and even that slight response is seriously divided. The first reviews that appeared in the French press in Montreal in 1945 were highly favourable. Jean Berand, for example, wrote approvingly of the novel's "don de sympathie" and its interest in national unity in *La Presse*, and, Abbé

Arthur Maheux, in a bilingual review in *The Gazette* entitled "A Masterpiece: Un Chef d'oeuvre," was enthusiastic about Mac-Lennan's "generous and intelligent effort" and his "marvellous success" in solving "our national problems." A few later commentators praised the novel on similar grounds. Jean-Charles Bonenfant, for example, who wrote a regular feature in *La Revue de l'université Laval* on "Les livres canadiens-anglais" commented there in 1950 that in studying "le problème des relations entres les deux grandes races du Canada," MacLennan "l'a fait avec beaucoup d'objectivité," and that his novel "crée une atmosphère fidèle" (742). In a subsequent article he added that "on souhaite plus que jamais que toute l'oeuvre de MacLennan soit traduite en français." Echoing some of the English-Canadian critics' greater enthusiasm for *what* MacLennan has to say than for his gifts as a novelist, Bonenfant adds that "[son oeuvre] est typiquement Canadien car, comme on l'a dit avec raison, MacLennan n'est pas un écrivain qui situe par hasard ses intrigues au Canada, mais c'est avant tout un Canadien qui, en second lieu, écrit des romans" (1951, 54).

MacLennan certainly speaks of his novel as having had an excellent reception in French Canada. "It took on with the French," he told me in 1987. "They were absolutely wild about it." He was vividly aware, too, that the story of Athanase Tallard's lonely struggle against the overwhelming majority of French-Canadians had a striking echo in historical reality in the furor over Senator T.-D. Bouchard in 1944. Bouchard had publicly criticized education in French Canada, and was not only fiercely and virtually unanimously denounced in the French-Canadian press as a result, but was also hounded from his $18,000 post as president of the Hydro Commission. In a note appended to the typescript of *Two Solitudes* in the McGill University Rare Book Library, MacLennan writes:

I finished the book and mailed it to Duell, Sloan & Pearce on (I think) August 29, 1944. Within a day or two after that, I recall, M. Bouchard was dismissed from his office as Minister of Roads in Quebec [*sic*] because of criticism made in his maiden speech (in English) in the Senate at Ottawa. It was a speech criticizing French-Canadian education, and the key factor in Bouchard's dismissal was an elliptical speech made by Cardinal Villeneuve in Saint-Hyacinthe. I remembered at the time thinking how similar was his fate to that of old Athanase Tallard. After the novel was published, M. Bouchard wrote me a letter complimenting me on it and noting the same point.[3]

The extreme unpopularity of Senator Bouchard within Quebec, whose speech was referred to as "vomitings" and who was considered as having excluded himself from his nationality as a French-Canadian (Wade 1968, 1108), certainly suggests a similarity with Tallard, and it apparently won MacLennan's novel at least one more French-Canadian admirer. The similarity, however, also suggests that *Two Solitudes* might itself likely come under fire.

In one case this is indeed what happened. The review by Albert Alain that appeared in *Le Devoir* on 15 April 1945 damned *Two Solitudes* for a poorly developed thesis and for a false and misleading depiction of French Canada. The unilingual and Protestant Mac-Lennan had in fact only the slightest personal knowledge of French-Canadians and of Catholicism — he had depended almost entirely on Ringuet's novel *Trente Arpents* and on conversations with a French Protestant colleague at Lower Canada College for his understanding of French Canada. "Le grand malheur," wrote Alain, "c'est qu'un tel livre donnera une très fausse idée du Canada français et catholique à des lecteurs de langue anglaise et non-catholiques au Canada et aux Etats-Unis."

The negative response to the novel in French Canada cannot, however, be measured solely by a rare instance of outright criticism. Far more telling is the fact that, in spite of Bonenfant's enthusiasm and in spite of some early interest by a Quebec publisher, the novel was not translated into French until 1963 and even then the translation was published in Paris. The first French edition to appear in Quebec was published in 1978. Alec Lucas, the only English-Canadian critic to have considered the French-Canadian response to the novel, comments that Paul and Heather's marriage may have caused the nineteen-year delay in publishing a French version, since French-Canadians see this marriage as a symbol of the assimilation of the French by the English (20).

Notwithstanding the almost complete separateness of the French and English literary worlds of Canada, critics of English-Canadian literature would do well to consider the implications of French-language criticism of *Two Solitudes* and especially of French

Canada's general lack of interest in the novel. Ben-Zion Shek has considerable insight into these very questions, but though his remarks have been published in English, they have not had any discernible effect on MacLennan's English-Canadian critics. And yet the questions surrounding the novel's impact in French Canada are of considerable importance. They cast the English-Canadian critical consensus about the worthiness of what MacLennan has to say in the novel — and especially its too ready identification of Paul as a French-Canadian — in a new light.

Once the English-Canadian critics' grand claims for MacLennan's understanding of Canada and particularly for his admirable conception of French Canada are undermined, what remains of the importance of the novel? Arguments for its importance have hitherto been based principally on what it has to say about Canada. If this "matter" is found wanting, what is there to justify its status as a classic of Canadian literature? The answer to this question requires an appreciation not only of what MacLennan has to say — of his matter — but of the extent to which, in *Two Solitudes* as in any work of fiction, the manner of writing matters. It is time to re-read *Two Solitudes*.

Reading of the Text

INTRODUCTION

Two Solitudes was published a few months before the end of World War II — on the eve, as it were, of what seemed sure to be a bright new day. Extravagantly high hopes were attached to the new start the world would be able to make once the war ended. The years of the Great Depression that darkened everyone's memories of the 1930s were gone. The Fascists who had dominated the international scene for more than a decade were clearly being routed. Repressive and conservative elements seemed to have had their day. This was keenly felt in Canada, and it was felt with particular vividness in Quebec, where all the most conservative elements of the Anglo-Scottish commercial élite worked in cahoots with the most conservative elements of French-Canadian society to ensure their own continuing ascendancy.

If many Canadians took heart from the spirit of the 1940s, they were further inspired by the wartime upsurge of Canadian nationalistic feeling. Shrugging off the vestiges of its colonial status, Canada was emerging from the shadow of Great Britain to become a nation among nations. It became urgent as never before to define Canada, to consider the kind of nation it had been and was and could be, and to affirm national unity. There was really little more than the semblance of unity in the 1940s, for French-Canadians had showed a distinct lack of enthusiasm for what they considered "England's war." There was, however, immense relief that the country had managed to avoid a replay of the crisis over Conscription that had so gravely divided French from English-Canadians during the first World War in 1917–18, and many Canadians were prepared for the first time in their history to believe in the real possibility of a Canada united *a mari usque ad mare* — from sea even unto sea. The time was ripe for a vision of Canada. This is the historical context within which the enormous impact and indubitable importance of *Two Solitudes* can best be understood.

Set principally in Quebec and in Montreal, concerning itself explicitly with the relationship between the French and English of Canada from the Conscription crisis to the outbreak of World War II, *Two Solitudes* is a novel about separateness and about unity. Articulating what "hundreds of thousands of Canadians felt and knew" — as MacLennan himself later put it — about the divisions in Canadian society (*Scotchman's Return*, 266), it concludes in 1939 with Paul Tallard marrying Heather Methuen and with a nation apparently marching off to war again in unity. "Love consists in this," the poet Rainer Maria Rilke wrote in the letter that provided MacLennan with the title for his novel and with its epigraph, "that two solitudes protect, and touch and greet each other" (Cameron 1981, 177). And in what does the unity at the end of *Two Solitudes* consist? Many of his English-Canadian readers have thought his imaginative solution to the problem heavy-handed and didactic; they have not hesitated, though, to approve of MacLennan's vision of national unity.

Two Solitudes is a long novel — 412 pages in most editions — in four parts; it spans a period of 22 years and, though it is set mainly in the village of Saint-Marc-des-Érables and in Montreal, it extends its ambitious reach across Canada, into the United States, to Europe and to the Far East in its attempt to provide an adequate context for understanding Canada. A sprawling work, in other words, but one to which MacLennan himself has provided a succinct introduction in his Foreword.

Here he explains that Canada has two official languages, that some of the characters in the novel "are presumed to speak only English, others only French, while many are bilingual." He emphasizes the separateness of the two cultures in his comments about the different names French and English use to refer to themselves and to each other. But in his affirmation that his novel includes both those languages and cultures, he promises to transcend separateness in this "novel of Canada."

MacLennan's choice of "Two Solitudes" as his title is brilliantly evocative. To his chagrin, however, it has from the outset evoked not the unity but rather the separateness of French and English Canada.

It is profoundly ironic that the title of a novel intended to affirm unity should, as Cameron shows, be firmly identified with the gulf that divides the two (1981, 188–89).

The novel is indeed imbued with duality in its subject and in its very fabric. After all, this is not only a novel about two cultures in Canada; it is really two novels — the one an epic narrative about Athanase Tallard who tries and fails to reconcile French and English, the other a *Bildungsroman* chronicling the maturation of his son Paul in whom the hope for reconciliation between French and English and for national unity supposedly lives on.

The epic opens in the fall of 1917 when the passage of the Conscription Act has divided English- from French-Canadians and provoked the most serious crisis in post-Confederation Canadian history. Athanase Tallard, a member of Parliament representing the rural Quebec riding that includes his ancestral village of Saint-Marc-des-Érables, has isolated himself politically by voting for Conscription. In due course he is socially isolated too when, at the suggestion of a shrewd English-speaking businessman, Huntly McQueen, and despite the opposition of the priest, Father Emile Beaubien, he tries to develop the village economically. Unable to reconcile the powerful opposing forces of French and English Canada, he dies a tragic figure.

The novel's focus of attention shifts to Paul Tallard in the *Bildungsroman* that follows his father's death. Half French and half English — Paul's mother Kathleen is a unilingual English-speaking Montrealer of Irish descent — Paul grows up to be an ideally bilingual and bicultural Canadian man, educated partly in French and partly at an élite English Protestant private school, at the Université de Montréal and then, since he has become a writer and he wants a better grounding in English literature, at Oxford. His marriage to the anglophone heiress Heather Methuen meets with vehement opposition from her mother Janet and from Huntly McQueen, who persist in considering him a French-Canadian, and it is hailed by MacLennan as the marriage of English and French Canada.

MacLennan wanted to transcend duality in his symbolic affirmation of unity in *Two Solitudes*. Criticism of his novel has focussed a great deal of attention in the intervening years on the causes of his failure to convey this message as effectively as he evidently wished. The message itself is widely considered worthy, but as a novelist he is typically regarded as not quite up to the task he has set himself.

His *matter* is considered important but his *manner* is found wanting. The relative weakness of Paul's characterization and the general collapse of MacLennan's narrative in Parts III and IV of the novel are the formal problems most commonly cited in efforts to explain why the novel falls short of greatness.

Rather than perpetuating the distinction between matter and manner, however, our reading of the novel views MacLennan's manner and his matter as profoundly interconnected. Instead of assuming that his matter is fine and that all the difficulties stem from his manner, our reading will re-examine both together.

The language of the novel — MacLennan's use of language as well as his choice of language — will provide a starting point in an appreciation of the inseparability of form and content. What message, after all, does MacLennan's language convey?

There are other questions that suggest the need to read the form along with the content. What does MacLennan's choice of genres have to tell us? And how are the genres in which he writes related to the way in which he depicts his characters? A consideration of the connection between genre and characterization in the novel shows that the difficulties his readers have with Parts III and IV of the novel and especially with characterization should be attributed not to any dramatic change in MacLennan's approach but to the very fact that it remains largely the same as it was in Parts I and II. The uneasy mix here of boldly drawn characters and a realistic narrative is most clearly seen in MacLennan's handling of Paul Tallard.

MacLennan may seem evenhanded in his treatment of the French and English of Canada, but this is an impression created by reading the content separately from the form of his narrative. What he explicitly says is indeed fair enough. An analysis of the structural asymmetry of his novel, however, reveals his own ethnocentric bias against his French-speaking and Catholic *concitoyens*.

And in MacLennan's preference for unity over separateness, what is his vision of unity? In what does this love consist? Do lovers not risk losing their own separate identities? This is what concerned Rilke. He was convinced that love consists in a certain distance between lovers — and that it cannot consist in mutual assimilation or in the subordination of one party to the other.[4]

Ever since the Conquest, French Canada has been afraid of "losing" itself, of being assimilated into the vast English-speaking sea of

North America. Its survival as a distinct society has depended on protection of its language, its culture, and its institutions, all of which, during the period that MacLennan focusses on in *Two Solitudes*, were the responsibility principally of the Roman Catholic Church.

Some of the thoughts attributed particularly to Father Beaubien and to Marius indicate that MacLennan has some intellectual appreciation of the French-Canadians' fear of assimilation. Father Beaubien, however, is depicted as narrow-minded, Marius as a racist and a fanatic. Not one significant character identified with French Canada's self-affirmation is treated sympathetically. For all his intellectual grasp of the issues involved, MacLennan's novel rides roughshod over the French-Canadian fear of assimilation. In his panoramic introduction to the novel in chapter I, indeed, where he identifies the Ottawa River with Protestant Ontario, the Saint Lawrence with Catholic Quebec, it is ironically the *Ottawa* that is described as merging and losing itself around the "pan" of Montreal Island before the "mainstream moves northeastward a thousand miles to the sea" (1-2).

As even the most matter-of-fact account of his narrative reveals it is not the Ottawa that risks losing itself in his vision of Canadian unity. In several important ways Paul is quite unrepresentative of French Canada: his parentage, his education, his apparent lack of religious belief, his unwillingness to return to Saint-Marc, his experience of Europe, the fact that he could be mistaken for an Englishman, and his aspirations as a novelist who writes in a tradition of English literature and presumably in the English language. His nationalist half-brother Marius, indeed, is the only character in Parts III and IV of *Two Solitudes* who can be at all plausibly identified as a French-Canadian, and his role is small. In the end MacLennan marries Paul to Heather, asks us to believe that their marriage represents the union of French and English Canada, and, to top it all off, identifies this symbolic marriage as Canada's best hope for unity.

There are Canadian novels both in French and in English that conceive quite nicely of a marriage between a French-Canadian and an English-Canadian. MacLennan himself even does a creditable if hardly an exemplary job of it in his depiction of the marriage between Athanase and Kathleen. His treatment of the marriage between Paul and Heather, however, is overwhelmed by his vision of national unity.

Two Solitudes is very much a product of its time in its denunciation of the old Anglo-Scottish commercial élite of Montreal (F.R. Scott was one of the few readers of the novel to complain that MacLennan had been too easy on the robber barons [Cameron 1981, 391]). It is very much a product of its time, too, in its criticisms of the role played by the Catholic Church in Quebec — which became the subject of some heated debate in Quebec during the 1940s and 1950s. And it is very much a product of World War II in its affirmation of Canadian nationalism.

MacLennan is deeply suspicious of French-Canadian nationalism — as Alec Lucas comments in a nice understatement, "Somehow [Marius] seems to have had little favour with the author" (29) — without showing any awareness that his own Canadian nationalism exposes him to some of the same criticisms he levels against Marius. This too is a product of the 1940s, for MacLennan associates French-Canadian nationalism and particularly Marius's gifts as a demagogue with Nazism and Adolf Hitler.

Looking to the future at the end of *Two Solitudes*, MacLennan seems anxious for change. Especially when his novel is viewed in the context of widespread English-Canadian ignorance about and prejudice against French Canada, MacLennan is liberal in voicing French-Canadian nationalist feelings and aspirations. He does not share those aspirations, however, and an affirmation of French Canada's distinctiveness within Canada is more than MacLennan is capable of. In this also *Two Solitudes* is very much a product of its time.

THE LANGUAGE OF *TWO SOLITUDES*

Hugh MacLennan is critical in *Two Solitudes* both of the power of the Catholic Church as identified especially with Father Emile Beaubien and of English commercial power as represented by the Methuen family and by the shadowy figure of Sir Rupert Irons. Much of his novel's reputation for liberalism stems from the fact that MacLennan has been read as unusually sympathetic to French Canada. While recognizing that MacLennan was a member of the English-speaking élite of Quebec, Elspeth Cameron, for example, attributes his ready identification with the "underdog position" of

French-Canadians to MacLennan's own Nova Scotian background (1981, 165). The role played by the language of the novel contributes mightily, however, to the impact of *Two Solitudes* generally and to its effect on our sympathies for each of the two tribes particularly. MacLennan is, after all, writing in the English language and from the perspective of a unilingual if well-intentioned Protestant Canadian personally unfamiliar with French Canada. "I didn't know many French people at all," MacLennan said in the 1987 interview. MacLennan's own background is by no means as privileged as that, say, of Heather Methuen, but as the son of a successful Presbyterian doctor, as a Rhodes scholar and a Princeton Ph.D. in his own right, and as a schoolmaster at the élite Lower Canada College in Montreal, he has closer affinities with the English-speaking and Protestant Montrealers he writes about than he does with any of the French-Canadians. Liberal as he is, moreover, in the sympathies he expresses for some of his French-Canadian characters — and especially for Athanase Tallard — he is writing with authority and with confidence in the language that French-Canadians considered a part of their problem.

To understand how important this is, let us stand back from our knowledge that this is a classic of English-Canadian literature and, like MacLennan himself, view the situation that the novel presents from a distance. Consider the situation, as MacLennan himself articulates it, of a French-speaking and Catholic people in a Canada dominated since the Conquest by an English-speaking and Protestant population and resentful of the power this population has over them both politically (French-Canadians are in a minority in Canada) and economically (business is at the time controlled by English-Canadian interests).

"A minority in a country they considered their own," French-Canadians are, as Marchand the politician in *Two Solitudes* puts it, "almost powerless against an alien people who called themselves countrymen but did not understand the peculiar value of the French and did not want to understand it" (46). That value lies in their language, their religion, and their culture, all of which distinguish them from the English-Canadian majority. In their survival as a separate people the importance of the Catholic Church can hardly be overestimated.

French-Canadians' sense of themselves as a conquered people has never been far from the surface of Canadian history since General Montcalm perished during the Battle of the Plains of Abraham and New France was ceded to the British. The fact that MacLennan chooses to begin his novel at the time of the Conscription Act of 1917 brings this persistent and fundamental problem into particularly clear view. This piece of legislation, in Father Beaubien's view — and in this he speaks in the voice of French Canada — shows how the English provinces are forcing the Conquest on Quebec for the second time (5). French Canada's sense of oppression and its bitter resentment of English Canada are at their height. Liberal and well-intentioned as MacLennan is, his decision to take this almost fatally divisive issue as his starting point in a novel that is written in English and focussed mainly on the French and English of Canada has put him in a difficult position.

Certainly there are precedents for such writing about another culture. A classic model for the well-intentioned author writing in an alien language about a clash of cultures is that of Julius Caesar in his accounts of the Gauls, for example, in his *War Commentaries*. Caesar's is a distant, godlike approach — "All Gaul," he pronounces majestically by way of introduction, "is divided into three parts"[5] — and he was of course, in addition, a military man entrusted specifically with the subjugation of the barbarian people of transalpine Gaul. Caesar is not only writing in Latin — and in exemplary Latin at that, as any scholar of the language will have been taught — but he is therefore identified with the power of the Roman Empire that oppressed the Gauls.

This distinguishes Caesar's writing from that, say, of *Out of Africa*, by Karen Blixen, who used the nom-de-plume Isak Dinesen. This Danish baroness, though she was white and though she wrote in English, was loved by the East African tribespeople that she lived among and cared for, and after her death they named the town of Karen (which is not far from Nairobi) after her.

Hugh MacLennan is not an imperial military commander dedicated to the subjugation of French Canada on the one hand; nor is he a beloved member of the French-Canadian community on the other. He cannot be reviled as an imperialist, and there is no town in Quebec called Hugh. *Two Solitudes*, in other words, lies somewhere between the *War Commentaries* and *Out of Africa* in its account of the meeting of two cultures. MacLennan's use of language is not the only consideration in how well he manages the delicate balancing act required of him in *Two Solitudes*, but it is a consideration that should not be ignored.

The Power of Language

The importance of *Two Solitudes* has been associated primarily with MacLennan's theme of national unity. W.J. Keith puts this view of the novel succinctly in arguing that its matter is more important that its manner (1983, 575).

A re-reading of the novel reveals, though, that the manner in which the novel is written — its style — is indeed important. It is also indissolubly linked with its subject-matter.

The style of *Two Solitudes* is not important in the same way as one might argue that James Joyce's prose style in *A Portrait of the Artist as a Young Man* is important — or Virginia Woolf's in *To the Lighthouse*. It is indeed far from constituting any kind of aesthetic breakthrough. MacLennan's style is old fashioned rather than innovative, harking back to a literary past that was remote even in 1945 and that is certainly no closer to us today. But saying that it is archaic is not the same thing as saying that it is not important. Listen to the opening sentences of *Two Solitudes*:

> Northwest of Montreal, through a valley always in sight of the low mountains of the Laurentian Shield, the Ottawa River flows out of Protestant Ontario into Catholic Quebec. It comes down broad and ale-coloured and joins the Saint Lawrence, the two streams embrace the pan of Montreal Island, the Ottawa merges and loses itself, and the mainstream moves northeastward a thousand miles to the sea. (1)

The opening paragraphs go on from this point to provide a wealth of geological, meteorological, agricultural, geographical, and even cosmological information that with mythic overtones and no little magnificence enables his readers to place this "novel of Canada" into perspective, and the first section concludes as follows:

> But down in the angle at Montreal, on the island about which the two rivers join, there is little of this sense of new and endless space. Two old races and religions meet here and live their

separate legends, side by side. If this sprawling half-continent has a heart, here it is. Its pulse throbs out along the rivers and railroads; slow, reluctant and rarely simple, a double beat, a self-moved reciprocation. (2)

This is a prose untroubled by doubt. Thanks in part to the very archaic quality that ensures no one will mistake MacLennan for a member of the modernist literary avant-garde, his literary authority here at the beginning of *Two Solitudes* resounds powerfully and convincingly. MacLennan's own thorough classical education colours his prose style as deeply as it colours his breadth of reference.

His rhythms, his sonority, and his syntax owe more to the classical prose masters with which his education had familiarized him than they do to any of his contemporaries in English prose. Long combined or complex sentences abound, as do long, slow vowels, and chanting rhythms. The repetitive effect becomes hypnotic if not *en*chanting, as when MacLennan writes in measured tones about the land: "All the good land was broken long ago, occupied and divided among seigneurs and their sons, and then among tenants and their sons" (1–2) and, "Every inch of it is measured, and brooded over by notaries, and blessed by priests" (2).

MacLennan's narrative sweep, too, owes more to the great epics of Homer and Virgil than to any modern fiction. There is nothing this narrator does not know; his absolute omniscience encompasses everything in heaven and on earth. He seems to know so well what he is talking about when he writes of the rivers, of the ploughed land, and of the tundra, that we trust him when he writes of the northern lights flaring into walls of shifting electric colours "that crack and roar like the gods of a dead planet talking to each other out of the dark" (2). As a narrator he is godlike, so why would he not know about the conversations of these fierce Nordic gods?

Most of his other images here in this introductory chapter are of similarly heroic proportion. The great waterways from the Great Lakes to the Atlantic cutting through solid rock lead MacLennan to imagine a sword plunged through the rock like the sword of Arthurian legend, and savagely wrenched out again. The sun stares out of the sky "like a cyclops' eye." The ploughed land "looks like the course of a gigantic and empty steeplechase where all motion has been frozen" (1–2).

The effect of all this is of incontestable significance. MacLennan is writing his own Canadian myth, establishing the indigenous "legends" that live here "side by side," and on this basis setting the scene for a national epic about Canada, for a Canadian saga (2). There is no mistaking his heroic intent in this really astonishing opening chapter as he alludes to Greek and Roman mythology, the great national epics of Homer and Virgil, Arthurian legend and the Nordic sagas.

The novel moves on to focus instead on Father Beaubien and the other characters who gather in Saint-Marc in the fall of 1917, but it never relinquishes its formality and its monumentality. Fully conscious of its own importance, its language continues to be language appropriate to a heroic narrative. The principal characters are larger than life, their battles are the battles of their people, and at stake is the fate of a nation. MacLennan's narrator remains omniscient throughout, moving at will into the consciousness of whatever character he wishes most vividly to illuminate, and he continues throughout the novel to express himself with impeccable correctness in lofty and allusive language.

Even in dialogue MacLennan continues in the main to use proper, grammatical English with only the slightest concessions to the vernacular. With a few notable exceptions (the speech of humble French-Canadians like Frenette and Drouin, Yardley's "thet" and Athanase Tallard's occasional gallicism, e.g. "I have the high blood pressure," 28), MacLennan's characters, whether English or French, speak as though they were educated at Oxford. This can be demonstrated using dialogue chosen almost at random. The following interchange between McQueen and Tallard on the train from Ottawa is typical:

"Your son made quite a speech the other night."
Athanase stared at him. "What speech?"
"Didn't you know. I assumed you had seen the press reports. About a fortnight ago, or maybe less. In Montreal."
Athanase shook his head. "I hadn't heard about it. At the university? I believe he's a member of the debating society." (72)

Although the sentences are shorter and the writing more matter-of-fact here than in narrative passages, MacLennan's only concession to the vernacular is his use of contractions ("didn't," "hadn't," "he's").

Powerful as the language of *Two Solitudes* is, it is not enough to characterize it as powerful. Many a writer fired by anger can be powerful, and many a writer delighting in attempts to shock or to subvert established authority can also be powerful. In MacLennan's case, the power of the language he uses is neither angry nor mischievous. His prose exudes authority. In so doing it asserts its own importance. As his remarkable formality even in dialogue suggests, *Two Solitudes* does not relinquish its importance even for the sake of greater realism.

MacLennan may wish to further a liberal cause in *Two Solitudes* by portraying French-Canadians in sympathetic terms and by using characters like Father Beaubien and Marchand to express their view of themselves as a people oppressed by English-Canada. The highly conservative tone set by this majestic prose style, however, is one of several features of his novel that work powerfully against the impression of liberalism.

The people he mentions in this opening chapter are French-Canadians whom he associates with the "delicate" bands of their farmland and with "fences tilting towards the forest" (1–2) — with images of fragility. He may not intend to set himself up above them, but this is the effect of his powerful use of language. Unlike the French-Canadians, his villainous English-Canadian characters are in due course identified with a virtual god-like power.

MacLennan gently satirizes the powerful Anglo-Scottish businessmen he describes in the elevator of the Bank Building in St. James Street in chapter II of his novel, but in the process he clearly identifies them not only as "remote from the beings they governed," but as immensely powerful: ". . . if an accident had occurred between the first and second floors, half a million men would at that instant have lost their masters" (104). And after Sir Rupert Irons's death, Heather wryly explains his importance to a puzzled American by saying "But Mrs. Falconridge — it's almost as though God had died!" (396). The godlike narrator is accordingly identified with English commercial interests, and MacLennan's language links him with anglophone power over and against francophone weakness.

It would be unfair to leave the topic of the power of MacLennan's language in *Two Solitudes* without giving it credit too for its various and significant successes. MacLennan's eloquence here is not at all inappropriate for the national epic that centres on the fate of

Athanase Tallard: the heroic mode calls for heroic language. In addition, MacLennan's prose is not only measured but it can also be quite beautiful, especially in many of his extraordinarily effective descriptions of the passage of the seasons and of the rural landscape of Quebec. Consider, for example, this passage about Athanase's return home to Saint-Marc:

> The odours of spring were multiple in the evening: ploughed earth drying and cooling after sunset, gummy buds swelling to bursting point on bare trees, the flat smell of the river washing its banks high . . . . They passed the old stone mill, then the Tallard land came into sight and the row of poplar trees running straight as an avenue in France from the road to his own door. A great crow swooped overhead, coming down in a long loop from the top of a poplar to settle on a fence post, where it crouched black and reverent in the gloaming like a priest in prayer. Westward the last saffron light of the day lay over the Laurentians: sunset in Ontario, late afternoon in the Rockies, mid-afternoon in British Columbia. (81)

Such prose is highly conscious of language. It uses images effectively. It expresses the theme of *Two Solitudes* and MacLennan's hope for French-Canadians' sense of Canada as a whole admirably. It does not work well in the *Bildungsroman* where indeed its grandness can, as we will see, create some incongruous effects. Here in the epic, though, it works well. There is much to quarrel with in *Two Solitudes*, but the manner in which MacLennan writes in the epic is neither unimportant nor unimpressive.

English: The Language of Power

Two Solitudes is written in English. The fact that it almost completely eschews the use of French is more striking today than would have been the case in the past. *Two Solitudes* is, however, about the French and English of Canada and, more pointedly still, about the historical lack of understanding between them and the possibility of mutual respect and of harmonious co-existence. The novel's almost exclusive use of the language associated with the political and economic power of the English-speaking majority of Canada accordingly has some bearing on our reading of the novel.

On rare occasions MacLennan will use a French word, but these are exceptions, really, which prove the rule. When Tallard explains to Yardley and to McQueen that "his wife was in bed with grippe" (11) the French word comes as a surprise not only for its rarity but because of its unlikeliness: if he were to use the French term, Tallard would more likely say that his wife was in bed with "the grippe." A different surprise surrounds the use of French in the account of the sentimental attachment to France that is called on to help explain why Athanase votes for the Conscription Bill:

> Since the days when he had been a student in Paris he had retained a feeling that France stood behind him: French culture, French art, everything that made *la grande nation*. (73)

Though MacLennan is indeed using French here, he is using *French* French as opposed to French-Canadian French, and so the language does nothing to support French Canada's particular aspirations. This instance of using French serves rather to underline how unusual a French-Canadian Tallard is in his love of France. France, as MacLennan clearly knows, is at the time resented by many French-Canadians for its abandonment of New France and for its atheism. This is one of the reasons why French Canada feels none of the need to rush to the aid of France during World War I that English Canada feels vis-à-vis Great Britain. Father Beaubien, here too a voice of French Canada, "certainly knew that if a people deserted God they were punished for it, and France was being punished now" (6).

By now we have grown used to finding a plentiful use of French in Canadian literary texts, especially since Sheila Fischman's influential translation of *La Guerre, Yes Sir!*, as well as in most of the descendants of *Two Solitudes* — fiction by Mavis Gallant and Leonard Cohen, Scott Symons and Gail Scott — that chronicle relations between French and English and that use words, phrases, even sentences in French more or less plentifully to recreate some of the texture of life in Quebec.

As readers we are particularly aware of MacLennan's virtually exclusive use of English in dialogue. This is an all too true reflection of his time, for English was until recently the usual language of conversation between most anglophones and francophones. Mac-Lennan's apparent intention, however, was rather to right some of the wrongs that French-Canadians have suffered at the hands of anglophones than to perpetuate them. In his Foreword, moreover, he makes a special point of commenting on the fact that some characters "are presumed to speak only English, others only French, while many are bilingual." Apparently, though, no English-speaking Canadian in his novel ever speaks French unless — as in Yardley's conversations with the villagers in Saint-Marc — the individual addressed is incapable of understanding English. The conversations between Yardley and Athanase Tallard are particularly revealing in this respect, since these two men are bilingual and each is notably well disposed to the other's culture. At their initial meeting in McQueen's company they certainly converse in English, and Mac-Lennan gives no indication that this ever changes. Indeed, the fact that Tallard continues to use the occasional gallicism — as he invites Yardley to have dinner with him and "Madame Tallard," he says "It would make us both a very great pleasure" (31) — strongly suggests that the two men continue to converse in English even when no unilingual anglophone is present.

The effect of this, unintended as it presumably was, is to deny difference. Look at the effect, for example, of the end of the hail-fellow-well-met conversation that takes place between Yardley and Tallard just before the latter proffers the dinner invitation. Tallard has been expounding on the narrow-mindedness of both French and English in Canada:

"... And then you go to Ottawa and you see the Prime Minister with his ear on the ground and his backside hoisted in the air. And, Captain Yardley, you say God damn it!"
Yardley blew his nose loudly and Paul got to his feet and edged around the chair beside him. (30)

The discussion turns to the French-Canadians' feeling for the land, and Yardley tells Tallard "Man to man" that he has the same kind of feeling himself for the land. When Tallard then learns that Yardley too plays chess and that he even has a set of men he picked up in India with elephants in place of bishops, Tallard responds with "I prefer bishops. After all, the movement of the piece is diagonal" (31).

This is in every way a discussion that Yardley could have had with an English-Canadian. There is nothing to suggest that there is any cultural difference whatsoever between these two men, let alone that they are from two different language groups who happened at the time of this conversation to be disastrously at odds with each other. This is presumably what MacLennan intended, and he wants the rapport between Tallard and Yardley to suggest how close French- and English-Canadians could be and might be and in some cases are. It is all the more unfortunate, therefore, that this particular friendship is founded on conversations in English and on the fact that "Man to man" as they are, the joke they can share is at the expense of Tallard's church. How close would these two men be, one wonders, if Tallard were not anti-clerical?

MacLennan's liberal intentions, already undermined by his powerful use of language in *Two Solitudes*, are dealt a further blow by his virtually exclusive use of English and by his concomitant neglect and denial of the difference between anglophone and francophone Canadians. The French-Canadian need to affirm its identity as a small francophone and Catholic society in a vast English-speaking and predominantly Protestant continent is here given short shrift. In his big book about Canada's two solitudes Hugh MacLennan remains unrepentantly unilingual. In this too his novel is a product of its time — a time long before the Official Languages Act and long before Quebec insisted on its *"visage français."* Such hope as MacLennan can point to for *rapprochement* between the two calls on French-Canadians to speak English.

GENRE AND CHARACTERIZATION IN *TWO SOLITUDES*

The romantic French artist Eugène Delacroix in a painting entitled "Liberty Leading the People," which hangs in the Louvre in Paris, depicts Liberty as a serene but dishevelled heroine storming the barricades with the tricolour in her upraised arm. Her face is in profile, and her expression suggests both her confidence and the righteousness of her cause. The portrait works well, indeed brilliantly, in the context of revolutionary turmoil in which the artist presents it. It answers any question you would care to ask about revolution, and it does so more eloquently than any political treatise.

Let us imagine the effect, however, if we were to take this heroic woman out of her context and view her instead against a realistically depicted interior of a modern office environment. She has not changed, but suddenly she seems overdrawn, really ridiculous, because as a figure larger than life she is incongruously out of place in an ordinary everyday setting. Her presence raises questions that did not arise in the original painting and that cannot be satisfactorily answered. Why is this woman so inappropriately dressed? Does she work here? Why is she so expressionless?

The point here is that an artist's depiction of character should not be viewed in isolation. How brilliant — or otherwise — an artist appears in his portrayal of character is a function not just of skill but on the kind of context — the genre — in which the character appears. The same is true of a novelist.

No novel stands or falls on the strength of characterization alone. All sorts of other factors may come into play — the quality of the novelist's prose style, the narrative energy, the appropriateness of the narrative structure, the attention to detail, the liveliness of the narrator's perceptions, etc. Mainstream contemporary fiction about the circumstances in which individuals find themselves, though, depends largely for its impact on realistic characterization. As readers of such fiction, our perceptions of characterization in a novel — and of the quality of the novel as a whole — depend to a considerable extent on the skills of the novelist. How finely has the author drawn the characters? To what extent can we identify with the characters? Are their actions believable? These are some of the questions we ask of the characters in a novel, and our opinion of the novel will depend to a significant extent on the answers we give to such questions.

So important is effectively nuanced characterization in an appreciation of mainstream fiction, indeed, that it is easy today to lose sight of the fact that there exist entire genres of fiction in which the author quite rightly and appropriately pays little attention to the realistic and plausible depiction of individual characters. It is high praise to comment on the nuances in Alice Munro's depiction of Dell in *Lives of Girls and Women* or in Margaret Laurence's depiction of Rachel in *A Jest of God*. But what sense does it make to compliment Jesus of Nazareth for characterization in the parable of the Widow's Mite?

Is an emphasis on effective characterization not misplaced in *Gulliver's Travels*? And — to bring our examples into the twentieth century — what about *Animal Farm*? Would it not be missing the point quite dramatically to praise George Orwell for characterization? There are many fictions that do not depend on nuanced characterization for their effectiveness. Some, like Michael Ondaatje's *In the Skin of a Lion*, for example, are good in spite of ineffective characterization; others, like Mavis Gallant's novella "The Pegnitz Junction," are brilliant *because* characterization is mostly outrageous or caricatured.

Literary criticism is not the application of immutable criteria to any given text. While the skill of the writer probably always matters, that skill sometimes consists in knowing when *not* to focus on individual characters. It is the critic's job to judge when it is appropriate to compliment a writer on nuanced characterization, and when such comments would miss the point. If this is a novel in which the author appears to be interested in the realistic depiction of individual characters, then it may well be appropriate to consider how well she does this. If this seems not to be a concern of the author's, then it behooves the critic to consider other and more appropriate criteria for appreciating the text. This is where genre comes in.

When we talk about genres of fiction we simply mean what *kind* of fiction we are dealing with. Is this a work of science fiction? of romantic fiction? of dystopian satire? of historical fiction? of realistic contemporary fiction? These and all the other genres of fiction matter because each works in its own way. It makes as little sense to praise a work of realistic contemporary fiction for its beautifully realized bug-eyed monsters and its vivid evocation of Utopia as it does to praise a science fiction novel for being perfectly realistic. Our expectations of a heroic narrative along the lines of *The Odyssey* and *The Iliad* of Homer, say, or of *The Æneid* of Virgil, will certainly not be the same as our expectations of a *Bildungsroman* along the lines, say, of James Joyce's *The Portrait of an Artist as a Young Man* or Anita Brookner's *Hotel du Lac*.

This brings us directly to *Two Solitudes*, which has often been criticized for its unevenness and specifically for the relative weakness of characterization in the sections of the novel that follow the death of Athanase Tallard. Although we may justifiably choose not to excuse MacLennan on this account, it is worth acknowledging that what lies behind this problem is not simply a matter of characterization. It is rather a matter of genre, for *Two Solitudes* begins as an epic and, after the death of Athanase Tallard, becomes instead a *Bildungsroman* centering on the maturation of Paul Tallard and his development into a novelist. This means that the criteria that properly apply to the early sections of the novel are not applicable to the later sections. In particular, the style of characterization that is entirely appropriate at the beginning is as entirely inappropriate at the end.

Many of the most interesting works of fiction transcend any single genre and are effective precisely because they play with a variety of literary conventions. It is rare, however, to find a novel split, as *Two Solitudes* is clearly split into what are two different kinds of novels. Many of the difficulties that readers have had with *Two Solitudes* stem directly from this split and from insufficient awareness of how differently each of the two "novels" should be regarded.

Characterization in *Two Solitudes*, like MacLennan's majestic use of language, remains largely consistent throughout. The impression of relative weakness in characterization in the later sections, and especially the perceived difference between the (effective) characterization of Athanase Tallard, who dominates the first part of the novel, and the (weak) characterization of Paul, who dominates the second part, derives not so much from any real difference in MacLennan's approach to characterization in the two "novels" as from the fact that in the second part MacLennan is writing in a different genre.

Though characterization and language remain much the same, almost everything else in the novel is dramatically changed in the transition from heroic narrative to contemporary realism. MacLennan's characters are subordinated to his theme throughout *Two Solitudes*. This is what is needed in the epic, where too many individual idiosyncracies and nuances of personality would simply confuse the important conflicts, issues, and distinctions between the French and English of Canada that are MacLennan's main subject. The heroic narrative requires characters who are boldly drawn types — heroes and villains, fools and knaves. This, in the main, is what MacLennan provides. The change of genre after the death of Athanase Tallard, however, throws the simplifications and banalities, the implausibilities and inconsistencies of MacLennan's characterization into relief. What had been admirable and certainly necessary in the epic becomes, in the *Bildungsroman*, a flaw. And as in the example of Delacroix's Liberty, a figure that may well be considered heroic in the one context can all too easily look incongruous and perfectly silly in the other.

The Epic

MacLennan's approach to characterization is appropriate and effective in the early sections of *Two Solitudes*. In this epic chronicling the meeting of two mutually ignorant and in several ways mutually hostile people in the Quebec of the early twentieth century, he has chosen to centre his depiction of the French of Canada on the Tallard family and that of the English on the Methuen family. Although MacLennan's characterization is subtle enough that none of his characters personifies either evil or good, he does nonetheless have villains and heroes, and, true to the heroic mode, his villains tend to be physically unattractive and his heroes fine handsome individuals. The villains are those in each clan who are most intolerant of the other — Father Beaubien and Marius Tallard, Huntly McQueen and Janet Methuen — and the heroes are those most sympathetic to the other clan and most interested in a rapprochement of the two: Athanase and Paul Tallard, Captain Yardley and Heather Methuen. The several occasions on which the heroes and villains cross swords clarify the issues at stake in the novel and intensify the suspense over the outcome — and hence over the fate of Canada.

MacLennan's depiction of his principals is rarely neutral. Almost every detail in his account of their physical appearance, their character, their speech, and their thoughts contributes to the positive or negative impression of them that he wishes to create.

Father Beaubien is a good case in point. From his first appearance, this big, energetic man swishing through Saint-Marc in his black soutane is obviously a force to be reckoned with. Of Norman peasant stock, he has large features, big bones, "shoulders strong as a ploughman's," and eyes unappealingly described as "seemingly magnified by the thick lenses" of his glasses (3). While acknowledging that Beaubien feels responsible for every soul in Saint-Marc, MacLennan is highly critical of the priest's impact on the villagers, who have dug deep into their pockets to pay for his monumental new church. The reason the Dansereau place is up for sale, MacLennan reveals, is that its owner contributed heavily to the new church and is now in debt (8). Beaubien, however, is "not yet satisfied" (5). The church still needs better heating, a bell, and a statue of Christ "about twenty-five feet high, with a halo of coloured lights above the head" (5).

MacLennan has a particular interest in Beaubien's hands, which are "big," "brown" (3), and "powerful" (4). When he realizes Tallard has brought English-Canadians to the village, "suddenly [his] big hands flexed, open and shut" (8). He drops his hands to his sides and walks quietly down the path to see where Tallard is going. He frowns when he sees the carriage turning into the Dansereau property, and then stands for several minutes, "his hands folded under his cross now" (8). By the time "his solid jaw" (6) sets hard at the thought of the war and the English, the role he will play as stalwart, narrow-minded defender of the Church and of French Canada against the English has become clear.

Unattractive as is his depiction of Father Beaubien, MacLennan recognizes too the genuineness of the priest's concerns for his parish. No such consideration tempers the depiction of Marius Tallard, in whom the priest's fairly intolerant clericalism and French-Canadian nationalism are significantly intensified. The negative impression is again created with dispatch. Marius is no ordinary unsavory character and, not to put too fine a point on it, is the victim of literary character assassination in MacLennan's hands. At his first appearance in chapter 5, rummaging around in the Tallard house and talking to Kathleen, he is assailed for self-importance, for his sense of racial purity, for dishonesty, for lewdness, for his hatred of the English, and even for his interest in pornography.

Physically his face is "thin and pale, with high cheekbones underlined by shadows" and his eyes, though "large, like his father's," are "without any humour" and as he strains to read his father's manuscript in the bad light "a sharp line formed between his brows and shot up to his forehead where a single vein was visible under the skin" (34). When his political activities in the following scene reveal him as a fanatic and a demagogue, the picture of villainy is complete.

MacLennan's ostensible intention being to present the two sides of the Canadian equation fairly, why does he identify all the French-Canadians in his novel who are closely linked with French Canada's national aspirations and with the Catholic Church in negative terms?

This applies to the politician Marchand too, though he is a minor character in the novel, and it applies to the insufferably pious Marie-Adèle, Tallard's first wife, though she has been long dead by the time the novel opens.

The only French-Canadian of any importance who is depicted in positive terms is Athanase Tallard. Patrician (he is "tall," "finely drawn," with "aristocratic features," and he reveals distinction in the way he gestures "with his long hands" [10]), sophisticated, anti-clerical, bilingual, witty, pleasant (his eyes are "large and brown" and "they twinkled easily" [28]), and perfectly at ease with English-Canadians, he is contrasted in several significant ways with Father Beaubien, and the contrast invariably works against the priest. No paragon (he neglected Marie-Adèle on her deathbed) he is nonetheless depicted as heroic in his struggle to convince French-Canadians of the need to acquiesce with the Conscription Act and, in due course, he is depicted as tragic in his failure to bridge the two solitudes.

As much of the action of the heroic narrative centres on the village of Saint-Marc, English-Canadians play a lesser role here than do the French-Canadians. MacLennan's approach to the characterization of the principals of each tribe, though, is identical in both cases.

The most vividly portrayed English-Canadian is Huntly Mc-Queen, and he happens also to be the character portrayed in the most negative manner. An Ontario Presbyterian reared with the notion that French-Canadians are an inferior people, he has modified his view only slightly in the eighteen years he has lived in Montreal. When introduced on his visit to Saint-Marc with Yardley and Tallard he reveals his bigotry at every turn. He is condescending about Tallard's library ("Who'd have expected to find a library like this?" [12]) and, discussing the marriage of Kathleen and Athanase behind Athanase's back he tells Yardley "You never can be sure where you stand with people like these" (12). He has other unappealing characteristics — he's sly, manipulative, self-important, calculating, and ruthless — and, as is the case with other unsympathetic characters, his defects of character are expressed too in his physical appearance. McQueen's face is as round as a full moon, and though his features — his "dominant" nose, "firmly set" mouth, and wide, intelligent eyes — lend him "an expression of force," his body is "ponderously soft" and he walks with "a padding movement" (11–12). References to McQueen's obesity recur throughout the novel (in the train from Ottawa, for example, he makes a deprecating motion "with his chubby hand" [72]). Most damning of all, perhaps, in the depiction of this character based in part on William Lyon Mackenzie King, who had been Prime Minister of Canada for most of Hugh MacLennan's adult life when he was writing *Two Solitudes*, is that McQueen (like Mackenzie King) has a mystical relationship with his dead mother, and he talks to her portrait in his office daily.

Kathleen Tallard is a unilingual English-Canadian of Irish extraction who lives in Saint-Marc as Athanase's second wife and Paul's mother. As such she might have played a very interesting role in *Two Solitudes*. Here, after all, is a true instance of the marriage of a francophone and an anglophone Canadian; here too is an instance of an anglophone living among French-Canadians in a rural village. There are other features of Kathleen's portrayal that might have contributed importantly to the novel: unlike any of the other English-speaking principals she is a working-class woman, she is sexy, and she is Catholic. Any or all of these characteristics could have affected our reading of the novel and our impression of the hope for reconciliation between the two solitudes. MacLennan exploits none of these possibilities, however, and Kathleen remains largely unimportant to the narrative except inasmuch as she is responsible for ensuring that Paul cannot be viewed as a French-Canadian.

The retired Nova Scotian sea captain, John Yardley, who becomes the only English-speaking and Protestant Canadian ever to own land in Saint-Marc, is portrayed more sympathetically than any other English-Canadian character. If Tallard is the heroic French-Canadian attempting to bridge the two solitudes, Yardley comes closest to being his English-speaking counterpart. Bilingual, sympathetic to the French-speaking population, sharing their feelings for the land, respectful towards their Church (he even attends Mass in Saint-Marc), he is humble and friendly, and he always has time for children and for a good yarn. Like Tallard he is nearly sixty years old, they are equally tall, and though his eyes are blue (Tallard's are brown), behind his rimless glasses Captain Yardley's eyes also "twinkled easily" (11). His heroic mien — he is "lean" and "muscular," and he has "the relaxed awareness of a man who has lived most of his life in the open, and some of it close to danger" — is partly offset by ears that stick out rather "like fans on either side of his head" (11). This seems rather an endearing characteristic, however, far from the un-attractive physical features of the novel's villains. More interesting is the fact that Yardley has a wooden leg, and that this, far from being depicted as a deformity, provides further evidence of his heroic stature. He lost his leg, MacLennan reveals, thanks to a German raider off the coast of Australia: Yardley is a naval hero of World War I.

The Bildungsroman

MacLennan's approach to characterization does not substantially change after the death of Athanase Tallard: the novel's population continues mostly to consist of heroes and villains. The heroes and villains, though, are less evenly matched, and the lines between them are less clearly drawn than they were in earlier sections.

In a few cases these are the very same heroes and villains as in the heroic narrative: Captain Yardley, Huntly McQueen, and Marius are fundamentally the same characters as they were earlier in the novel, although they are relegated to the narrative sidelines. Two characters, Janet and Heather Methuen, assume considerably more important roles than hitherto — the former as a villain, the latter as a heroine — and one, Paul Tallard, becomes the heroic protagonist on whose maturation and development into a novelist the *Bildungsroman* focusses.

Serviceable and appropriate as MacLennan's techniques of charac-terization were in the early sections of the novel, they have some unintentionally comic effects in the *Bildungsroman*. It is always easier to portray heroic characters with large brush strokes and to ignore the unheroic details of their lives. This is more convincingly done with a narrative set in the past — like the early sections of *Two Solitudes* — than in fiction contemporary enough to prompt readers to draw comparisons between the lives of the heroic figures and the unheroic characteristics of their own everyday lives. And in the *Bildungsroman*, MacLennan is writing about the 1930s, a time within easy reach of his novel's 1945 publication date.

Janet Methuen's appearance in Saint-Marc had a sufficiently dramatic effect to ensure there would be no doubt at all about her villainous nature. This, after all, is the woman who turned in Marius to the military authorities when he trying to avoid conscription. Her role becomes considerably more important in the novel, however, once her daughter Heather gets involved with Paul Tallard. Her vehement opposition to their love affair and to their marriage is founded entirely on racial prejudice against French-Canadians (like the other English-Canadians in the novel — and, as we have seen, most English-Canadian commentators on the novel — Janet considers Paul to be French): "It would have been such an awful mistake," she tells Heather, "for you to have made — a mixed marriage like that. I'm quite sure he's quite a decent boy — among his own kind" (402). Outraged that Paul has turned down a job offer from Huntly on the grounds that the war would have started before he could get to British Columbia, Janet scoffs, "As if a French-Canadian would join the army anyway!" (402).

The combination of heroic mode and realistic narrative is particularly incongruous in Janet's opposition to Heather's involvement with Paul. When she learns that Heather and Paul have already married, Janet overreacts preposterously. "A low cry, half moan, issued from Janet's lips. . . . Her right hand clutched spasmodically at her left breast as if trying to reach through to her heart; then, like an independent claw, it jerked to her forehead . . ." etc. (403). Janet, it will turn out, is affected considerably less seriously than she pretends. MacLennan's handling of the scene, however, is unsatisfactory. Melodramatic and comical as his account of it is, he apparently intends it to be taken seriously. Heather, he tells us, "watched in horror" (403). The big final scene in which Paul stands up to Janet and effectively silences her is certainly intended to be taken seriously, and here too Janet's behaviour is overdramatized. In a "crisp and British" voice she orders Heather to "Come along" with her, and when Paul quietly insists they stay, Janet lifts "her hand to her cheek as if Paul had slapped it," her mouth opens and closes, and she stares at him, "her fingers clasping and unclasping on her purse" (409–10).

The problem here is that Janet — like McQueen and like Marius — is drawn as boldly in the *Bildungsroman* as in the epic. The more realistic depiction expected in a *Bildungsroman* is, however, an inappropriate context for characters with such exaggerated features.

In part this is a problem too in the characterization of Paul, on whom the *Bildungsroman* depends most heavily for its impact. Certainly he is loaded with heroic qualities. The son of a French-

Canadian aristocrat and a working-class English-speaking Montrealer of Irish extraction, he is perfectly bilingual and bicultural, modest, tolerant, liberal, and well intentioned. A star hockey player and an Oxford-educated novelist, physically strong and artistically sensitive, a local boy, a world traveller, and a critic of the old guard, Paul shares many characteristics with MacLennan himself. He is surely a match for Athanase Tallard in his impressive list of admirable qualities. The problem is not that he is relatively weak, as has often been suggested, but that MacLennan has made him the hero of a novel very different from the one in which his father appeared.

The *Bildungsroman* centred on his development concerns itself mainly with the possibility of change in Canada. The big conflict here is not between French and English. It is rather between the old and the new Canada. English-speaking retrogrades like Janet and Huntly and Rupert Irons are aligned with French-speaking retrogrades like Marius inasmuch as they all cling to the old prejudices. Opposing them all is a new wave of tolerance and liberalism that descends, as it were, from Yardley and from Athanase Tallard, and that is identified with Heather and especially with Paul.

As hero of the *Bildungsroman* Paul personifies the new Canada. In the process of chronicling the development and maturation of an individual character named Paul Tallard, Parts III and IV of *Two Solitudes* also chronicle the development and maturation of Canada. The novel that Paul finally embarks on is his own "Two Solitudes" — his own "novel of Canada" — even as it is the story of his own life.

The sophisticated self-reflexivity of this has been insufficiently appreciated in MacLennan criticism. It is a technique that prefigures Canadian post-modernism. The connections between it and, say, the narrative self-reflexivity in Michael Ondaatje's *In the Skin of a Lion* and in Gail Scott's *Heroine* will bear examination. (Each of these two recent novels is interestingly comparable to *Two Solitudes*, too, in others ways: Ondaatje's in its interest in ethnic relations and in a re-creation of early twentieth-century Canada, Scott's in its interest in English-French relations in Montreal.)

MacLennan's use of Paul's novel suggests the formal accomplishment of *Two Solitudes* has in some ways been underrated. Its thematic resolution of the French-English problem, however, is a mess. Paul cannot *both* bridge the solitudes in his own person *and* represent

French Canada. MacLennan is rightly viewed as having grossly overburdened the marriage of Heather and Paul with a meaning it cannot support. It can support little meaning. These two are, after all, just the two individuals most interested in a new wave: no historical opposition is symbolically reconciled in their union. Mac-Lennan's attempt to use the marriage to tie up the loose ends in English-French relations was a mistake.

THE TWO SOLITUDES IN *TWO SOLITUDES*

Much of the impact of *Two Solitudes* must be attributed to what has always appeared to be MacLennan's surprisingly even-handed treatment of French and English Canada. Certainly it is to his credit that he faces the divisions between the two squarely. The Conscription crisis on which the first part of his novel centres and the question of the economic development of French Canada by English-Canadian industrial capital bring some of the most profound and emotionally charged questions of French-English relations in Canada into sharp relief. Identifying the French principally with the Tallard family and the English principally with the Methuen family, MacLennan creates the impression that he is depicting their many differences objectively and fairly. This impression of symmetry depends on what Mac-Lennan explicitly says about the two solitudes. The way in which each is worked into the structure of his narrative, however, is far from symmetrical.

French Canada: The Tallard Family

The vast majority of French-Canadian families in the first half of the twentieth century were rural, economically underprivileged, multitudinous, unilingual, and devoutly Catholic. At some point, owing to economic necessity and in spite of the best efforts of the priests to keep people on the land, many French-Canadians moved from the country into the city where they suffered severe dislocations and continued economic hardship.

This is hardly a description of the family of Athanase Tallard. The Tallard family's roots, certainly, like those of the most French-Canadians, are in Normandy, they speak French, they live in a rural village, and they are Roman Catholic. Furthermore they share with all French-Canadians an awareness of a history and a culture that distinguishes them sharply from English-Canadians. But the Tallards' experience differs so profoundly from that of most French-Canadians that they can hardly be considered typical.

Few French-Canadian families, certainly, were privileged as the Tallard family in *Two Solitudes* is privileged, few would be as well-educated and as bilingual, few would have as lively a tradition of anti-clericalism, as few children, and as strong a sense of Canada as a whole. Fewer still would have been headed by a Member of Parliament, and of these practically none would have argued in Ottawa in 1917 in favour of conscription.

Of course the family is also closely connected with the very ordinary rural community in Saint-Marc, it is powerfully influenced by Father Beaubien, and it includes the pious Marie-Adèle, the French-Canadian nationalist Marius, his unilingual and uneducated wife Emilie, and their many children. Diverse and profoundly divided within itself as it is, it seems all the more unusual.

MacLennan's choice of the Tallard family to represent French Canada, however, is in some ways astute. MacLennan was of course limited by the fact that, unable to converse in French, his knowledge of French Canada was all second hand, but this would have limited him in depicting any family. The Tallards certainly do not come close to being whatever could be considered a "typical" French-Canadian family, but in all their diversity and with all their divisions, the Tallards are in some ways more *representative* of the poles of French-Canadian experience than a more "typical" family could be.

During Athanase's lifetime, this divided family is presented from the point of view of its articulate *paterfamilias*, who is an extraordinary French-Canadian able to see his immediate family and his people with some of the clarity and critical detachment of an outsider. The distance that characterizes Athanase's attitude to French Canada is especially evident in discussions between Athanase and Yardley. When Yardley wonders that Athanase doesn't just stay in Saint-

Marc, Athanase shrugs his shoulders and says "Maybe I'd get bored if I were here all the time" before he goes on to describe other French-Canadians' feelings about the land:

"Our people feel about the land the way they do in Europe, I think. It would be sentimental to say they love it, but I tell you one true thing — they look after it better than they look after themselves. They hoard it." (31)

This detachment is a strength in the novel inasmuch as no "typical" French-Canadian would be able to explain French Canada as well to an outsider — not only to Yardley but also to MacLennan's English-speaking readers across Canada and the United States. Athanase's free-thinking and his exposure to English Canada as a Member of Parliament permit him to compare the two people, to appreciate what makes French Canada different, and also to view it critically. When he comments, for example, on French Canada's too-heavy reliance on politics as a means of exercising influence ("They talked too much while the English kept their mouths shut and acted" [18]) he is speaking from a point of view that no ordinary French-Canadian could have shared.

Tallard's detachment, however, is also a weakness in the novel. It means that the most important, admirable, and likeable French-Canadian character in *Two Solitudes*, the one on whom we as readers rely most heavily for our view of French Canada, is distanced from almost everything that matters to French-Canadians. He tells Yardley,

"Here the Church and the people, are almost one and the same thing, and the Church is more than any individual priest's idea of it. . . . The Church, the people, and the land. Don't expect anything else in a rural parish." (28)

Spoken by an anti-clerical French-Canadian aristocrat with little feeling for the land ("I'm not important to the land," he shrugs. "I just own it" [30]) this may be informative but it works against any growth of sympathy and real understanding of French Canada as a whole.

All that is typical about French Canada — and most notably the

Church and its extraordinary role in the survival of the French language and of French-Canadians as a distinct people — remains without any sympathetic spokesman. Those characters who are closely identified with the Church and French-Canadian national affirmation — Father Beaubien and Marius especially, but also lesser characters like the politician Marchand — are treated with precious little sympathy. MacLennan certainly does reveal some understanding of the concern for the future of French Canada that motivates such men. The best account of French Canada's predicament certainly comes through them and MacLennan's occasional adoption of their point of view rather than from Athanase Tallard. When Marchand's thoughts turn on the effect of the anti-conscription meetings held all over Quebec in 1917–18, he allows MacLennan quite effectively to express some of the reasons for French-Canadians' frustration and anger:

> . . . where oratory was being sprayed out like an anaesthetic to deaden the French-Canadians' bitterness because they were a minority in a country they considered their own; because the pressure of the eight English-speaking provinces east and west of them, and of the United States to the south, made them feel they were in a strait-jacket; because now, with the world gone crazy, they were almost powerless against an alien people who called themselves countrymen but did not understand the peculiar value of the French and did not want to understand it. Marchand felt all this sincerely. (46)

Such understanding of French-Canada as this might further is, however, seriously undermined by MacLennan's grossly unsympathetic depiction of Marchand as a calculating and opportunistic populist who despises people ("My God," he mutters. "Some of the bums they let in here stink when they sweat!" [47]). Comments about French-Canadian fears and aspirations elsewhere in the novel are similarly undermined by the characterization of Beaubien as a bigot and of Marius as both a fanatical demagogue and a professional failure.

MacLennan could have retained the strengths of Tallard's detachment while doing a better job of portraying the mainstream of French Canada and its nationalists. Tallard does not and cannot speak properly for French Canada; the novel's close identification of French

Canada with Tallard in fact robs French Canada of any powerful voice. And this is not a problem that dies with Tallard. The fact that his second wife, Kathleen, is an English-speaking Montrealer of Irish extraction means that Paul Tallard is half English and largely educated in English — and that in the second of the "novels" that make up *Two Solitudes*, the *Bildungsroman*, the aspirations of French Canada are identified solely with the pathetic figure of Marius. MacLennan's failures here are serious. They suggest his sympathy for French Canada and its aspirations is severely limited.

English Canada: The Methuen Family

English Canada is mainly depicted in *Two Solitudes* through the stiffly restrained retrogrades like Janet Methuen and Huntly Mc-Queen on the one hand and the easy-going progressives like John Yardley and Heather Methuen on the other. Though this is a less varied (and a smaller) family than the Tallards, it appears on the surface as though MacLennan is equally critical of each of these two great families and equally appreciative of those few of its members who are able to transcend the limitations of its people.

Typical of English Canada only in being English-speaking Protestants whose ethnic roots go back to the British Isles — to England, Scotland, and Northern Ireland — the Methuens are at least as privileged as the Tallards, they are considerably wealthier, and as they are quite cut off from any less privileged class of people, they are not representative of English Canada in the same way that the Tallards are.

MacLennan is clearly much more at home in the drawing rooms of Montreal's Square Mile and of Westmount than he is in the *dépanneur* in Saint-Marc or in Tallard's ancestral home. In his depiction of the Methuens he therefore has much more scope for criticism, and he is sure enough of his ground here that he can afford to go into considerable detail (as in the account of the elevator full of powerful businessmen in chapter 11, and of Huntly McQueen's dinner party in chapter 31), which he eschews in his relatively tentative and vague accounts of French-Canadians.

While he satirizes the retrograde Methuens for their stiffness and awkwardness in social situations and while he mocks Huntly in particular for talking to the portrait of his dead mother, MacLennan's criticisms are not extravagant. He creates at least two excellent opportunities in the novel to damn the retrogrades, but takes full advantage of neither.

One arises after Janet Methuen, acting on information from Daphne, hands Marius over to the authorities and thus ensures he will be conscripted. Disgraceful as her father, Yardley, thinks this is — he is moved to apologize publicly on her behalf in Saint Marc — the incident is robbed of effect by the fact that Marius has been characterized in such unfavourable terms that he is unable to prompt much sympathy, and — even more significantly — by the fact that the hero of the novel, Tallard, favours Conscription. In these circumstances Janet may fairly wonder what she did that was so disgraceful. Her comments about French-Canadians when Yardley asks her about Marius reveals her at her most bigoted ("It's time they were brought to heel" [187]). Her bigotry, certainly, comes as no surprise. What has been lost in this incident, though — as in the treatment of the Conscription issue throughout — is an opportunity for Mac-Lennan to show that he takes French-Canadian fears and aspirations seriously.

A similar opportunity is lost in MacLennan's handling of the central issue of the epic: Tallard's plans for the economic development of Saint-Marc. This was originally Huntly McQueen's idea, but Tallard gets deeply involved in the plans and in the financing because he feels it is important for French-Canadians to develop their own resources. Father Beaubien is opposed to the plan, and his arguments deserve more careful consideration than Tallard gives them:

"Let me tell you something," Father Beaubien said. "In the place where I was first curate no one owned anything but the English bosses. There were factories there, but the people owned nothing. They were out of work a quarter of a year around. . . . They saw English managers throwing money about while prices rose and they grew poorer. They blamed the priest for not being able to do more for them." His voice rose. "Always that's the story! You accuse me of disliking the English. As a people I have nothing against them. But they are not Catholics and they do our people harm. They use us for cheap labour and they throw us aside when they're finished. I won't let you do that here, Mr. Tallard. I won't let a man like you spoil this parish." (167)

This argument is left unanswered and, in the thick of the battle between the two men, Beaubien himself diverts attention from this powerful argument by bringing up Tallard's unseemly behaviour on the night of Marie-Adèle's death. Here again, though, MacLennan is presenting an issue of crucial importance to French Canada, and here again he has his hero aligning himself with the English.

The novel does not bother ever to give Beaubien his due for being quite right about the effect development will have on Saint-Marc, but the development eventually goes ahead without Tallard, and such passing references as are made to the village later on leave no doubt at all as to its fate. "It's pretty near a good-sized town now," Yardley tells Heather in 1934, "all filled up with unemployed and every other damn thing a town needs to feel itself important" (300). And Paul knows it would be "senseless" to return to Saint-Marc. Polycarpe Drouin is dead. Frenette is an old man now: "after years of being his own master he had been compelled to give up his forge and now was just another employee of the factory":

> Saint-Marc was not a village any more; it was a small factory town, and some of his father's land had been turned into a golf course by the company. Instead of playing checkers in Drouin's store, coming into it informally whenever they felt like it, the villagers now played organized bingo games in a community hall on Saturday nights. (372)

Any power such accounts might have to depict English business generally and Huntly McQueen particularly in the role of villain is seriously undercut by Tallard's responsibility in furthering the cause of development of the village.

The fact that the most forceful expressions of French-Canadians' frustration and bitterness in the novel are undermined by being associated with intolerant or unsavory characters means that even villainy on the part of English-Canadians appears excusable.

That MacLennan is critical of the extraordinary influence of the Catholic Church in French Canada is not unexpected. But he has seemed to many readers to be at least as critical of the English-speaking commercial élite, and indeed of the limitations of English Canada more generally. The protagonist of the epic, moreover, is a sympathetic and enlightened French-Canadian gentleman who is both a passionate Canadian patriot and the spokesman for some of Mac-Lennan's most pointed criticisms of Canadian society. When Captain Yardley points out that a man who has anything to do with brewing beer or the Canadian Pacific Railroad in Montreal seems to be " 'something like a duke is in England,' " Athanase Tallard responds:

"He is certainly the big fish in the little puddle. We French, we watch them and smile. . . . The trouble with this whole country is that it's divided up into little puddles with big fish in each one of them. I tell you something. Ten years ago I went across the whole of Canada. I saw a lot of things. This country is so new that when you see it for the first time, all of it, and particularly the west, you feel like Columbus and you say to yourself, 'My God, is all this ours!' Then you make the trip back. You come across Ontario and you encounter the mind of the maiden aunt. You see the Methodists in Toronto and the Presbyterians in the best streets of Montreal and the Catholics all over Quebec, and nobody understands one damn thing except that he's better than everyone else. The French are Frencher than France and the English are more British than England ever dared to be. And then you go to Ottawa and you see the Prime Minister with his ear on the ground and his backside hoisted in the air. And, Captain Yardley, you say God damn it!" (30)

In passages like this one MacLennan — like Tallard — appears to be above the divisions, objective, unusually perceptive, and thoroughly admirable. He seems, in short, to be unusually fair and liberal in his depiction of Canadian society.

The impression of symmetry in his depiction of the two clans is not entirely an illusion. It derives from the similar roles played out by individual members of each in a kind of Canadian allegory of

French-English relations. The heroic spokesmen for Canadian unity are Athanase Tallard on the one hand and Captain Yardley on the other. The villainous reactionary and separatist elements in each case are represented by intolerant individuals who, though not in fact members of the family, stand *in loco parentis*. In the case of the Tallard family this powerful figure is Father Beaubien, who as the village priest embodies the values associated with Tallard's pious first wife, Marie-Adèle, who died giving birth to Marius. In the case of the Methuens, the analogous figure is Huntly McQueen, who as a scion of the English-speaking commercial élite of Montreal embodies the values associated with Harvey Methuen, and who assumed Harvey's role in the family as Janet's advisor and as a parental figure for the two girls after their father's death during World War I. The older child in each family — Marius, Daphne — is associated with this reactionary element, while the younger — Paul, Heather — is associated instead with tolerance and reconciliation.

MacLennan is walking a fine line here. He needs to establish the similarities between the two clans firmly in order to create an impression of even-handedness. At the same time, though, this is a human drama. Complete equality between the two is neither necessary nor desirable, and MacLennan could be accused of being mechanistic if he had gone any further than he does in establishing similarities between Tallards and Methuens. His characters must have sufficient individual characteristics to save them from being perceived entirely as allegorical figures. As a group, moreover, the composition of each clan needs to be distinct enough from the other to avoid creating the impression that the one is simply the mirror of the other.

It is in walking this line that MacLennan falters. His characters are, in the main, convincingly enough individuated for the kind of epic narrative in which they move. Although it is true that some of the best passages in *Two Solitudes* are those that articulate the differences between these two clans and that seem to hand out demerits fairly equally, the impressions created of the French and English of Canada are not solely formed by what is said about them and by the similarities in the composition of the two extended families. MacLennan's use of English raises questions about his apparent objectivity. Then too there are significant differences between the two clans that, in spite of Captain Yardley's best efforts, tip the balance in favour of

English Canada. On the complicated balance sheet of accommodation between the two, French Canada gives far more than it gets.

John Yardley and Athanase Tallard

The best way of judging this is to consider the attitudes, behaviour, and social status of the two men of good-will, Captain Yardley and Athanase Tallard. Both about 60 years of age, both with twinkling eyes, both bilingual, and both tolerant of the other culture, they represent the best of each of the solitudes.

Yardley's behaviour in Saint-Marc is admirable: he attends Mass, speaks French with the unilingual villagers, provides work for one of them, and apologizes to them on Janet's behalf after she has turned in Marius to the military authorities. Although he lost his leg fighting the Germans earlier in the war and he makes no secret of the fact that he favours Conscription, he avoids arguing the question in Saint-Marc. His personal charm and his sensitivity to the villagers' concerns is such that he manages to overcome their deep-seated suspicions of the English. Unshakably if not very devoutly Presbyterian — "My old father, he whaled the Presbyterian catechism into me when I was a kid, so I'd feel mighty peculiar if I went permanent to another church" (29) — he has a courteous relationship even with Father Beaubien, and it is rumoured he gave the priest twenty dollars for his poor box (21).

These are the novel's finest examples of English-Canadian accommodation of French Canada. Their significance should not be understated. It cannot properly be judged, though, in isolation, and here the comparison between Yardley and Tallard is revealing. For Tallard not only uses English as a matter of course with English-Canadians whether or not they are bilingual, he is married to a unilingual English-Canadian, and his sons are both bilingual. Where Yardley's political and religious convictions are typical of an English-Canadian, moreover, Tallard has sided *against* his people on Conscription, he is anti-clerical, and in due course he converts himself and Paul to Protestantism.

Yardley — the best that English Canada has to offer — is likeable and sympathetic, he says the right things, and he makes the right gestures. His accommodation of French Canada is personal and admirable. Tallard, though, has in addition taken historic strides in identifying himself in political, religious, and cultural terms with the English. His accommodation of English Canada is heroic. The relative status of these two gentlemen in their respective families is a further consideration. The apparent symmetry that characterizes the composition of the two families is undermined by some significant differences. The most notable of these, as none of the Methuens is French, is the fact that Kathleen Tallard is English-Canadian, which means that Paul is half English. The different roles played by Athanase and Yardley are, however, also worth noting. The fact that Athanase is head of the Tallard family provides him with a central place in the novel's depiction of French Canada. His already enormous accommodation of English Canada is accordingly lent further significance by his status. Yardley, on the other hand, is an eccentric grandfather on the fringe of the Methuen family, and the significance of his admirable behaviour towards the villagers is accordingly diminished in the novel's depiction of English Canada.

An Imaginary Anglo

Let us imagine how differently we would read the novel if there were indeed a centrally important English-Canadian in *Two Solitudes* whose sympathies for French Canada were a match for Athanase's sympathies for English Canada.

This imaginary protagonist would not only speak French with French-Canadians whether or not they were able to speak English, but he (in 1917 he has to be a man to play this role) would also be married to a unilingual French-Canadian Protestant called Catherine, his second wife. Our hero — let's call him Alfred Tarlton — has an adult son called George by his first marriage to Mabel. Catherine leads a rather bored and certainly a lonely existence in our hero's ancestral Ontario village of (say) Little Markham, where the Presbyterian minister, Mr. William Goodwell, is an Orangeman and where not another soul speaks French. Alfred is a member of Parliament, away from Little Markham for much of the time, so Catherine, who can communicate with no one else in the village, has almost single-handedly taught their son Martin flawless French. Under a great deal of fire not only in English Canada but also in French Canada (where he was not thought to be wholehearted) for voting against the Conscription Act, Alfred considers the untold benefits that will accrue to Little Markham if he instead devotes his energies and his remaining wealth to the creation of a French school. Many of the people of Little Markham are very concerned, though, at his stand on Conscription; Mr. Goodwell himself is appalled, for several of his parishioners have already been killed in France for lack of sufficient Canadian reinforcements; and Alfred has a violent argument with his older son George, who is determined to join up. Years later, a further disagreement over the involvement of a Roman Catholic bishop in his plans for a local French school brings Alfred's unpopularity in Markham to a head. Financially ruined over the school issue and bitterly disappointed at the ingratitude of the people of Little Markham, Alfred moves to Toronto and converts to Catholicism, reverting to the religion of his ancestors moments before he dies.

Implausible as this imaginary Anglo may seem in 1917–21, and even taking the profound differences between the two cultures into account, such an English-Canadian is no more unlikely than Athanase Tallard. The distance between Alfred Tarlton and John Yardley should be clear, and as Yardley is English Canada's best hope, there evidently is no English-Canadian in the novel who comes even close to being a match for Athanase. MacLennan's treatment of the "two solitudes" only appears to be symmetrical.

French Canada Forgotten

The profound asymmetry that marks the epic is very clearly in evidence in the *Bildungsroman* that follows. Athanase, of course, is dead by the end of Part II of the novel. Saint-Marc, the villagers, and the Catholic Church disappear altogether. MacLennan still discusses French and English as though they both mattered equally to his narrative — he goes to some lengths to show that the English-Canadian characters (Yardley, Janet, McQueen) regard Paul as

French-Canadian and therefore that the marriage of Paul and Heather is a symbolic marriage of French and English Canada. As before, however, what is explicitly articulated about French and English is quite different from what his narrative conveys about them.

In his focus on the development of the half-French and half-English Paul Tallard in Parts III and IV, MacLennan has given up on French-Canadians almost entirely. English Canada's most tolerant representative in the *Bildungsroman* is Heather Methuen, but she has no personal contact that we know of with French-Canadians, and she quite understandably has doubts over Paul's French identity. "You're still French — aren't you, Paul?" she asks while they are travelling through the Gaspé, to which he replies with a laugh that "I certainly would be if I stayed long enough in a place like this" (361).

The only French-Canadian character of any importance to appear in Parts III and IV of *Two Solitudes* is Marius, who appears briefly and only in order to allow MacLennan to insist on the dangers of (French-Canadian) nationalism. His uniqueness in these sections of the novel forces the reader to identify the aspirations of French Canada with him alone. The fact that Marius is depicted in uncompromisingly negative terms — MacLennan caricatures him not only as fanatical and racist, but as a personal failure — accordingly excludes any possibility of understanding French Canada's aspirations.

While Marius is overdrawn, the point here is not that he is implausible. Certainly there were fanatical and frustrated nationalists in Quebec during the 1930s with close ties with fascist movements. There were, however, also moderate elements in French-Canadian society that would have feared assimilation and that would have wanted to ensure the survival of the French language and culture in Canada, and these are not adequately represented in *Two Solitudes*.

There is some slight suggestion in the portrayal of Marius's wife Emilie and of the villagers of Saint-Marc that sympathetic characters might have legitimate concerns over the future of French Canada. These characters, though, play such an insignificant role in the novel that the whispers of moderation are drowned out by the shouts of fanaticism. By identifying French Canada's need for self-affirmation almost exclusively with an unsavory extremist, MacLennan further undermines the possibility of any serious consideration of this important issue.

It is not necessary that a novelist provide a fair and balanced depiction of society. In the main, indeed, we look to a novel not for the sociological accuracy of its account of the world we know but for the imaginative power that its author brings to bear on the creation of a fictional world. MacLennan's use of historical events and circumstances in *Two Solitudes* and his declaration in the Foreword that his is "a novel of Canada" invite comparison between his depiction of Canada and the reality of Canadian society in the early decades of this century. The impact of his novel cannot, however, properly be appreciated in terms of considerations of sociological accuracy any more than it can properly be appreciated solely in terms of aesthetic considerations.

MacLennan's treatment of "solitudes" other than the French and English of Canada provides another reason to question the overwhelming extent to which MacLennan has been praised for what he has to say about Canada and more or less severely criticized for how he says it. If MacLennan's conception of Canada finally leaves little room for French Canada, it has even less sense of other social groups. When the substance of what MacLennan has to say — and what he fails to say — about these groups is considered in isolation, it is hard not to conclude that the "matter" of *Two Solitudes* is further weakened by its denigration and exclusion of various other "solitudes." The issue is complicated, however, by the very fact that this is indeed a novel and that its form contributes massively to its impact. In fiction, manner matters. And the "matter" in *Two Solitudes* is significantly strengthened by the manner in which MacLennan uses imagery to develop his own impressive conception of "the ultimate solitude."

The Other Solitudes

Taking MacLennan's claim that his is "a novel of Canada" seriously, let us for the moment imagine the effect a reading of *Two Solitudes* would have on a reader who does not live in Canada and who knows little about it other than what she learns from MacLennan's novel. This reader would get the impression that almost everyone in Canada is either of French or of British extraction. This has never been the case, and in a comparison between MacLennan's simplified view and the reality of Canadian society, *Two Solitudes* must appear correspondingly limited and misleading.

The Native People of Canada

The Native people of Canada receive the barest mention in his novel. In the vast sweep of MacLennan's introductory chapter, which incorporates everything else from the land that is "brooded over by notaries and blessed by priests" all the way to the northern lights cracking and roaring "like the gods of a dead planet talking to each other out of the dark," the Indians and Inuit who lived in Canada long before either French or English arrived and who continue to live here are conspicuous by their absence. "Nothing," MacLennan writes, lives on the tundra "but a few prospectors and hard-rock miners and Mounted Policemen and animals and the flies that brood over the barrens in summer like haze" (2).

When the Indian is mentioned it is in a discussion in the general store in Saint-Marc among the villagers about Captain Yardley, who speaks French "with terrible grammar and a queer accent mixed with many English words . . . worse than an Indian, Polycarpe Drouin said." Though used in the context of the French-speaking villagers' liking for Yardley, who is "very different from their notion of an English-Canadian" (21), this remains a slur.

The only other reference to the Native people of Canada, this time about Eskimos, is made by Heather Methuen. Even if Janet and Huntly "knew of the marriage," she thinks, "it would still be no easier to make them understand what passed in her mind than it would be to converse with Eskimos" (386). The point here is to stress the gulf between her own values and those of her family — and her class. In the process, though, the Eskimos are treated off-handedly, and the gulf between them and Heather is underlined.

Acceptance of Ethnic Diversity

Some of the ethnic diversity of Canadian society is suggested when mention is made of a portrait of a "Negro" girl that Heather has in her room. The artist is a Czech painter Heather has met. "It was a bitter portrait, the breasts sagging and the ribs slatted like scantlings, one bony hand on a hip and a hopeless expression on the tired face" (287). Janet Methuen is "horrified" when she sees the painting, which convinces her that Heather is making "some very unfortunate friends." Janet gets Huntly to investigate the Czech and is only partly mollified to discover he is a quiet little man with a wife and three children and very little means; she hopes none of her friends will chance to see the picture hanging in the house (287).

As well as noting the presence in Montreal of a Czech and perhaps also of the woman who is the subject of the portrait, the discussion of the painting, like Heather's reference to the Eskimos, is evidently intended to show one of the profound differences in values that distinguish her from the typically retrograde members of the English-speaking social élite of Montreal, especially Janet and Huntly. Its effectiveness is offset, however, not only by the virtually complete exclusion from the novel of Canadians of other ethnic origins, but also by some perfectly illiberal remarks made in the novel about members of other races.

The main culprit in this, surprisingly enough, is Captain Yardley, and perhaps the racism of his remarks has been overlooked by readers of the novel because Yardley is so tolerant and sympathetic where French-Canadians are concerned. Consider, however, his story about the time he and the man he calls "Luke" (i.e., Luc) Bergeron and "the blackest nigger thet ever came out of Barbados" were in Saigon in 1877 (26). "[W]hen Luke stepped onto the dock in Saigon he was a mighty surprised man, because outside the coolies all the white men talked French" (26). The point of the story is to explain Yardley's attraction to Saint-Marc (where he claims he thought he might find Luke) and his bilingualism (he and his companions ended up spending four years on a French vessel running the China Seas), but the disparaging terms in which he has referred to the black man and the Vietnamese, realistic as they may be, undermine his reputation for broadmindedness.

This is not an isolated instance. One of the yarns Yardley tells young Paul is full of such racist remarks. " 'Well, anyhow, one time a dirty little dago lad we had on board, he took out his knife and slit the nigger's moustache,' " he tells the boy, and goes on to describe how the "nigger" " 'jumped the dago, and the skipper heard his neck crack clear above the hatches' " (66). Paul, MacLennan assures us, "laughed because the story had no sense of disaster the way Captain Yardley told it" (66).

On his deathbed Yardley remembers an old Chinaman who had tried to induce him to smoke opium, and who had also attempted to interest him in rice-bowls and wash-drawings:

> He [Yardley] had been ashamed then of liking useless things which were merely beautiful, for he had been given a strict upbringing. And also — Yardley smiled as he remembered — he had somewhat despised them, and for no better reason than because he had possessed enough physical strength to beat up that Chinaman with one hand. (351)

We would not be surprised to hear such comments from someone as narrow-minded as Yardley's daughter Janet Methuen. Their illiberal effect, however, is compounded by the fact that they are made by Yardley, one of the novel's most admirable characters, and the fact that these remarks are allowed to stand without any comment from the narrator links not only Yardley but MacLennan himself rather more closely with the values of a Janet Methuen than might otherwise have been imagined.

Élitism

Limited as it is in respect to the ethnic makeup of Canada, and questionable as it is in its treatment of other races, *Two Solitudes* has been charged too with creating a skewed impression of Canadian society in its focus on the social élites.

Though MacLennan's general identification of English and French Canada with the extremely privileged Methuen and Tallard families does seem at least in part to support this view, the formal qualities of the work need to be taken into consideration here.

Even in terms of content alone it should be remembered that each of these families also includes less privileged individuals. In the case of the vastly wealthy Methuens only Captain Yardley is a man of modest means, while the Tallards include a wider range of social types. Kathleen Tallard comes from a working class background in Montreal, and when Athanase is ruined, all of the Tallards suffer the economic consequences — though he manages to get through university, Paul finds doors closed to him during the Depression. When the community of Saint-Marc that forms a kind of extended Tallard family is included, the picture broadens further. The villagers are all ordinary peasant people, and Father Beaubien himself is of extremely humble origins.

Considering MacLennan's own inability to converse in French and his lack of personal familiarity with French-Canadians, his depiction of their lives is remarkably good. Brief as it is, for example, Mac-Lennan's fine account of Emilie's father's sufferings (52) and his depiction of village life in Saint-Marc throughout the early sections of the novel are more substantial and far better than his depiction of English-speaking working classes, ethnic immigrants, or Native peoples. As he has acknowledged, MacLennan in large part owes the richness and plausibility of his portrayal of French-Canadians to his reading of Ringuet's *Trente Arpents*. It is ironic to consider how convincing his depiction of French Canada is compared to his depiction of ordinary Canadians who are *not* francophone. If anyone had previously written about the English-speaking working classes in Verdun and Pointe St-Charles, about the lives of immigrants in Montreal, or about Canada's indigenous populations, perhaps Mac-Lennan would have done a better job with such social groups too.

The argument that MacLennan's vision is socially elitist is really an example of how an analysis based purely on a consideration of the content of a novel can provide a misleading impression of its overall effect. For MacLennan's use of social élites is intimately connected with his choice of the epic genre in the story of Athanase Tallard. Valuable as it would have been if he had rounded out his account of Quebec society more fully, MacLennan is here writing in the heroic mode, and the conventions of such writing are such as to allow the deeds and misdeeds of the great to stand for those of an entire society.

Charges of elitism stand a better chance of being sustained in the *Bildungsroman*, where the conventions of realistic fiction come into play. Even here, though, this is hardly an issue likely to strike many readers of the novel with great force. The only characters who are still privileged at this stage are the members of the English-speaking élite of Montreal, and if the novel does not denounce them as vehemently as it denounces the likes of Marius, it certainly treats them critically.

"The Ultimate Solitude"

Like the French and English of Canada, these various "other solitudes" are all social groups. A quiet and an entirely different kind of meaning, however, is actually given to the term "solitude" in the novel itself, where it refers to individual angst. What MacLennan does with his notion of "the ultimate solitude" not only offsets some of the negative effects of his dismissive handling of other social groups, but it also contributes importantly to the novel's accomplishment in formal terms.

Simplistic as MacLennan's conception of Canadian society may be, his handling of the intimately personal "ultimate solitude" has the effect of establishing bonds among characters who are French and English, male and female, grand and humble. In a novel concerned above all with transcending separateness with unity, and which has been both widely praised and occasionally damned in terms that suggest it does this only in its content, these bonds strongly suggest that the formal qualities of MacLennan's work have been underrated.

The term "ultimate solitude" is used memorably of Captain Yardley in a scene of such central importance to the formal connections established in *Two Solitudes* that it needs to be quoted at length. Struck by a sense of poignancy as he watches Paul walk home, Yardley thinks wistfully of how wonderful everything would be "if you could be always among people who knew no fear. Among people who never groped at their neighbours like blind men in a cave" (68). As a sailor and as a ship's master, Yardley has "known solitude in strange places":

He was persuaded that all knowledge is like a painted curtain hung across the door of the mind to conceal from it a mystery so darkly suggestive that no one can face it alone for long. Of ultimate solitude he had no fear, for he never let himself think about it. But he knew that if he once started, fear would be there. (68)

This passage is elaborated on further in Yardley's memories of an afternoon in the tropics when he had leaned over the taffrail watching the "fish gliding through ten fathoms of sunlit water below."

Sharks and barracuda moved in their three-dimensional element, self-centred, beautiful, dangerous and completely aimless, coming out from a water-filled cavern hidden beneath the promontory and slipping under the ship's keel, fanning themselves for seconds under the rudder, then circling back into the cavern again. A moment he saw them in the golden water and then they were gone, and the water was as if they had never been there. The first mate had come to him for an order and broken his contemplation, but the memory of the hour had never left him. Self-centred, beautiful, dangerous and aimless: that was how they had been, and he could never forget it. (68–69)

It concludes with Yardley's thoughts about his life in Saint-Marc, where he has been "lonely," and about Paul, for he knows all too well "the constant tug of war between the races and creed in the country" and "that they would all fight over" the boy.

This scene, and particularly its haunting central passage about the tropical fish, is the key to some of the most important connections that the novel establishes.

These tropical waters with their dangerous fish are contrasted not only with other big fish in Tallard's account of Canada as "divided up into little puddles with big fish in each one of them" (30), and with Sir Rupert Irons's conception of a merger, which is "about the same as a shark's when it encounters a herring" (108), but also with the sweating soldiers Tallard and McQueen see on their way to Halifax, where these relatively small species will be crowded into the hold of a ship "like fish in a can" (74).

If the images of fish establish links among different groups and classes of Canadian society, the emphasis on loneliness and fear in this scene furthers such associations. Not only Yardley but Kathleen,

Athanase, and Paul are all described in terms of their loneliness, and in this they are no different than the humblest characters in the novel — from Luc Bergeron (27) and Ovide Bissonette (62) to the prospectors on the tundra who, hearing the world is at war, "could stand the solitude no longer," head south, and fade into the army (411).

The extent to which *Two Solitudes* is indeed haunted by the spectre of personal loneliness and suffused with nameless fears is considerable. Kathleen knows that, in Saint-Marc, "I'll always be alone" because the villagers have never forgiven Athanase for marrying her (89). On his deathbed Athanase receives the last rites from a Catholic priest. In response to a question of Paul's about this Yardley says, " 'Your father being a Catholic . . . well it means he got lonely and wanted to be what he'd been all his life, I guess. Or maybe it means something else so big I can't understand it' " (241). Kathleen remarries years later, and during the ceremony, "[i]f loneliness is a man's inability to share his feelings with another, Paul has never been as lonely in his life" as he is now (275).

The sadness of *Two Solitudes* is never more clearly expressed than in the account of Paul's stay in Athens, when he feels the city itself surrounding him "like a giant presence of loneliness":

> It was no new feeling; most of his life he had known it, and now it was recurring again like a periodic disease. This loneliness of all large cities, the solitary man reading his newsprint, the instinctive hope that there is new life just around the corner if you go to it, but around the corner always the same emptiness, the urgency which makes you want to prowl always a street further . . . . (337)

The disease of loneliness afflicts human beings of every race, colour, creed, and class and thus ironically but appropriately creates a unity based precisely on separateness. MacLennan's imagery throughout *Two Solitudes* skilfully insists on the very connections that his novel wishes to further. *Two Solitudes* would have been a better book if MacLennan had trusted his tale enough to let it speak for itself here, but he is anxious to find a cure for loneliness, and the only possible cure is love. It is to love that we now turn.

Love consists in this,
that two solitudes protect,
and touch, and greet each other.

Rainer Maria Rilke

Only love can succeed in bridging the solitudes. Love is the only possible cure for the disease of solitude that so many of the characters in *Two Solitudes* suffer from. In his novel's grand attempt to transcend separateness and to celebrate unity, everything, finally, hinges on love. As we have just seen, MacLennan has formally developed the rich — and unifying — implications of a sense of solitude very effectively. It is all the more disappointing, therefore, to find him failing to work them through to the end.

The association between solitude and the love between a man and a woman itself is nicely presented around the only mention of the term "two solitudes" ever made in the text of the novel.

Paul, who has been away from Canada for five years working and studying at Oxford and discovering his vocation as a novelist, is feeling homesick in Athens. He is reading a letter from Heather, who has been working in New York and who wishes he were there with her. He imagines what it would be like if instead she were in Athens with him. Suffering from "the loneliness of all large cities," he wonders as he sits in a café in the Place de la Constitution "if Heather had ever felt as he did now. Two solitudes in the infinite waste of loneliness under the sun" (337–38).

Effectively as this particular passage picks up many of the threads of the novel, from its title and its epigraph to its many references to personal feelings of loneliness, the novel's treatment of love is otherwise unimpressive.

The reason for this is not simply that MacLennan has burdened the love between Paul and Heather with meaning. While it is indeed true that their love is loaded with meaning, love is often loaded with meaning in fiction, sometimes to brilliant effect. The reason for MacLennan's failure here is that the meaning that the love between these two characters is asked to bear is at odds with the meaning of the *Bildungsroman*.

The love of Paul and Heather is asked to represent the union of French and English Canada. This is the meaning clearly indicated by the coinciding meanings of the term "two solitudes," which refers to the love between individual human beings on the one hand and to the French and English of Canada on the other. It is supported by Captain Yardley's comments about Paul and Heather each being the victim of the two racial legends within Canada (301), by the obvious identification of Heather as an English-Canadian, and by English-Canadian characters' ready identification of Paul as a French-Canadian.

The view that the marriage between Paul and Heather symbolizes the "union" of French and English Canada, however, is incompatible with the several other qualities of Parts III and IV of *Two Solitudes*. The genre and characterization of the *Bildungsroman* and its narrative structure argue strongly against the very meaning MacLennan wishes this marriage to convey.

Genre and Characterization

The fact that Parts III and IV of *Two Solitudes* constitute a *Bildungsroman*, a realistic genre of fiction centred on the convincing development of Paul significantly affects our reading of his romance with Heather. As this is a genre that begins and ends with the individual, it is clearly going to run into serious difficulties when the protagonist is instead asked to assume a meaning as a symbolic or allegorical figure representing an entire society. MacLennan himself was aware of this difficulty:

> I wrote of a legend; this was not easy, and required endless rewriting, as the characters, once I had made my choice, had frequently to be rejected if their own lives interfered with the design I had felt at the beginning was true. (Cameron 1981, 188)

Paul, the character whose development is of such importance to the *Bildungsroman*, combines in his person many of the characteristics of English and of French Canada. " 'It's a tribal custom in Canada to be either English or French,' " he tells Heather. " 'But I'm neither one nor the other' " (304). To some extent Parts III and IV of the novel capitalize on this in some eloquent passages dealing with his personal attempts to come to terms with his unusual and in some ways difficult situation, and particularly in his realization that he can write a novel that is not only about Canada but also quite directly about his own experience (375).

Certainly Paul cannot plausibly be identified as a representative of French Canada, and MacLennan succeeds quite convincingly in tracing Paul's development as a man who is neither French nor English — and who is both French and English. The irony here is that his success in depicting Paul in bicultural terms ensures that Paul's marriage to Heather cannot be considered a marriage between French and English Canada. To the extent that it is nonetheless evident that MacLennan wants their union to be meaningful, it has quite unfortunately to be considered as suggesting the assimilation of French Canada.

Structure

Structurally the novel has in Parts III and IV all but forgotten its original interest in the relations between the French and English of Canada. Marius's shrill voice is the single voice of French Canada still heard here, and it is heard seldom, while the voice of Janet Methuen sounds considerably more often and more powerfully than was the case in the epic. With no equivalent representation from French Canada and virtually no interest in French-English relations, the *Bildungsroman* accordingly furnishes few opportunities to focus (as in the epic) on the gulf separating the two tribes. Its concern, properly enough, is with Paul's development into a young man who is critical of the mistakes of the past, optimistic about the possibility of improvement, and intent on playing his own part in effecting change as a novelist. The *Bildungsroman* accordingly shifts attention away from the failings of the Janets and the Huntlys as intolerant English-Canadians to their failings as members of a retrograde older generation.

In the heat of the conflict between the English and French of Canada that develops in the epic, a love affair between an English-Canadian and a French-Canadian could have meant a great deal. The closest MacLennan comes to depicting such a love is his account of the marriage of Athanase and Kathleen, which lost its lustre years before the novel opens; and the mixture of attraction and repulsion that Marius feels for Kathleen. If ever passionate love between the two solitudes is needed it is here. With both tribes on the warpath, Janet Methuen falling in love with Marius, say, or Huntly falling in love with Emilie could have changed the course of history.

Next to such extravagant imaginings the love between Paul and Heather is tame indeed. Even if Paul really could properly be identified as a French-Canadian, the narrative's lack of interest in French and English Canada in Parts III and IV of *Two Solitudes* has undermined any importance that a marriage between an English- and a French-Canadian could have.

Solitude over Love

MacLennan's handling of the love between Paul and Heather is not only loaded with contradictory implications but it includes some of the most awkward and unsatisfactory scenes in the novel.

The love between these two individuals develops only in the last quarter of the novel and even then is the focus of attention only briefly since the lovers meet on no more than two occasions before Paul leaves Canada, and are seen together only for short periods after his return and their marriage. This is probably just as well, for MacLennan's forte is not writing love scenes. "What was love anyway," the narrator asks when Paul takes Heather's hands in his for the first time, "but a knowledge that you were not alone, with desire added?" (323).

With its last phrase tacked on as an afterthought, this sentence suggests MacLennan is in favour of love, but is not nearly so sure about desire.

At times it seems that this is because of a deep distrust of desire unaccompanied by love, which he sees as intensifying loneliness. In

77

Athens Paul exchanges a glance with the woman who is sitting at the next table, "and he knew he could have her if he wished." He decides he isn't "equal to that kind of loneliness today" (338).

This, however, does not explain Paul's avoidance of Heather, whom he supposedly loves. On their only day together before he leaves Montreal in 1934, they kiss. When he then lights a match and sees "wonder in her eyes," he exclaims,

> "Heather — don't! I . . . it's the one thing I'm afraid of."
> "Why Paul?"
> "Why? My God — don't underrate yourself."
> Her voice seemed far away. "I'm not afraid. Not now."
> He tore off another match, but he didn't light it. "Next week I'm going away. We may never see each other again. Let's remember that." (322)

What are we to make of this odd scene? What is Paul afraid of? His imminent departure — for five years, no less — provides no adequate explanation, particularly since he is leaving on his own volition and could return to Heather any time he chose. Does his hesitation have something to do with his awareness of the difference in wealth between them? MacLennan does not say, and the vehemence of Paul's reaction simply leaves an incongruous and somewhat ludicrous impression.

Shedding her impatience, Heather is satisfied with a chaste hug and then drives Paul home where he kisses her hand and suggests she might write to him. " 'Have fun, darling,' " Heather tells him as she releases the clutch of her car. " 'And take care of yourself' " (324). This is hardly one of the world's great passions.

Five years later, on the eve of his return to Canada, Paul's thoughts about what Heather and he would do on an evening together reveal more about the nature of their relationship. "He'd like to take her to dinner at the Grande-Bretagne," "sip wine until dark," and then "drive to the Akropolis in an open carriage. . . . The moon would rise enormous and round," and moonlight would touch the caryatids. "Heather had a body like theirs. . . . Her lines were female and fruitful in the memory." Will they touch? Well, yes. "They would stand touching each other while they looked across the dark plain where the Long Walls had run down to Piraeus." And then? (MacLennan is not, after all, an author who shies away from a depiction of sexual scenes, as his account of Kathleen's adulterous affair demonstrates.) Paul "would tell her how in the old days, when the triremes rounded the cape on their way home, the quartermasters seeing the first glint of sunlight from the spear of Athene on the Akropolis had raised their arms to salute the goddess" (335).

A love affair can be tentative and formal and still work. It can even on occasion survive some unintentionally comic effects. It must, however, be convincing, and the love between Paul and Heather is not convincing. How realistic is it to imagine that this love, based on some distant childhood memories and one evening and one day together should survive a separation of five years and result in marriage? And if the love between Paul and Heather really is in spite of appearance big enough to survive, then why do they not move heaven and earth to get together? And why is their relationship so unsexy?

In spite of many assurances that they do really miss each other when they are apart, their actions belie their words. After Paul's return to Canada they spend a short period together and get married before Heather goes off to Kennebunkport to be with her mother, and then Paul goes off to war.

Instead of presenting this affair in a manner that would leave no doubt that this, really, is love, MacLennan calls it love while presenting it half-heartedly and unconvincingly. Though he is never at his best in romantic scenes, the weakness of his handling of what should have been the climactic scenes of *Two Solitudes* is particularly striking. MacLennan manages, after all, to convey Kathleen's adulterous affair passionately if melodramatically. He manages to suggest some of the intensity of Marius's sexual interest in Kathleen.

These are relationships based, however, on desire. Love has little to do with them. And the relationship between Paul and Heather, though formal and distant, is one of love, with (a little) desire added. One source of the novel's lack of conviction in its presentation of this love may be the characterization of Heather, who is treated more like a caryatid or a goddess than a woman of flesh and blood. In this she is quite unlike Kathleen — who is depicted as indolent, sensual and sluttish — and equally unlike the woman at the next café table whom Paul knows he could "have." In order to affirm unity over separateness, *Two Solitudes* needs to affirm the possibility of a love that can bridge the solitudes. Moonlight touching the caryatids, and the quartermasters (significantly, Paul has himself been a quartermaster [331]) saluting the goddess are far from convincing images for such a love between a man and a woman.

Another reason for MacLennan's failure in his crucial account of the love between Heather and Paul is his use of two different narrative genres in *Two Solitudes*. The formality of Paul's imaginings in Athens, its classical allusions, its portentous use of language would not be out of place in the epic. All these characteristics are completely out of place in a realistic narrative, and at this crucial juncture in his novel MacLennan's account of the love affair wants to be sublime but succeeds only in being ridiculous.

A further consideration in our appreciation of MacLennan's failure to depict the romance effectively is a comment made much earlier in the novel. Athanase is supposed to have been a great lover of women in his day. At the end of his life, however, he finds it "[i]ncredible, that for most of a lifetime a man could imagine that beauty was enough, or that women could satisfy the ultimate solitude" (220). Athanase of course knows by this time that he has himself failed to find a way of reconciling the divisions in Canadian society. The idea that love is generally unable to "satisfy the ultimate solitude," however, seriously undermines any possibility that love might allow for a transcendence of separateness.

The novel's lack of conviction about the love between Paul and Heather then seems linked with some profound scepticism about the power of love. MacLennan may not have intended to suggest that solitude cannot finally be transcended, but this is what his half-hearted handling of love conveys. Love is not up to the challenge this "novel of Canada" presents. In spite of MacLennan's Herculean efforts, the form of *Two Solitudes* ultimately conveys the perpetuation of solitude.

CONCLUSION

Two Solitudes is a Canadian institution that has from the outset been venerated and excoriated. In the years since the wave of MacLennan criticism in the late 1960s and early 1970s, the novel has largely been taken for granted. Most English-Canadian literary critics have hitherto been most interested in MacLennan's themes and in the meaning of his work, only secondarily in his formal accomplishment as a novelist. Mac-Lennan's evident concern in *Two Solitudes* with issues of national significance has seemed to support such an approach, and the consensus has been that this is a novel seriously flawed in its form but undoubtedly important for what it has to say about the possibility of reconciling the differences between the French and the English of Canada. It is on this basis that mainstream critics have established *Two Solitudes* as a classic of Canadian literature.

And it is on this basis too that revisionist commentators have recently argued that MacLennan's reputation as a novelist has been inflated for nationalistic reasons — and have suggested throwing the baby of MacLennan's novel out with the bathwater of its nationalist message. These arguments have not yet been supported by any substantial re-examination of the novel, which has evidently proved far less interesting to influential critics today than it did twenty years ago. Fashions in criticism, of course, go hand in hand with fashions in writing. As the critical focus in Canada has shifted from themes and meanings to forms, the tendency has been to ignore MacLennan, and to focus rather on writers whose interest in language and form lends itself most readily to varieties of formalist analysis.

This study has considered how the formal qualities of *Two Solitudes* affect a reading of the novel. It suggests it is high time we revised our opinion of the novel. Certainly the novel is important, but it is important not for the worthiness of what it says. Of course it is flawed. Novels are mostly flawed, and the more ambitious the novel the more likely it is to be seriously flawed. It is easy to identify faults, and especially now that fashions have changed it is easy to dismiss and to ignore MacLennan's grandly ambitious novel. The loss, however, would be ours.

What MacLennan has done in *Two Solitudes* is attempt to find a form to accommodate the duality of the Canadian experience. This is the importance of his novel, and this is the basis on which it is rightly considered a classic of Canadian literature.

How successful he is in this attempt is a question that each generation will answer for itself. The conclusion to be drawn from this re-reading is that *Two Solitudes* is formally far more accomplished than has hitherto been suggested.

MacLennan's use of imagery is one characteristic of *Two Solitudes* that has been too little appreciated. It permits him to work the notion of "the ultimate solitude" into the fabric of the novel impressively. So convincing is he, indeed, in his writing about solitude that it is possible to imagine that if he had trusted his tale of separateness instead of insisting on imposing a spurious unity on the narrative, he might have succeeded in saying something true about the Canadian predicament — and in writing a great novel in the process.

His descriptive skills are considerable, and his prose shows a keen awareness of language. The majesty of his style, though too authoritative to please contemporary taste, is undoubtedly powerful in the epic if not in the *Bildungsroman*. Paradoxical as it may seem that a novel that constituted a breakthrough in the development of Canadian literature when it was published in 1945 should be written in such a conservative and even archaic style, MacLennan's writing is quite appropriate for a work that in Parts I and II sets out to create a kind of national myth. The difficulties with his writing really emerge only at the end of the novel where his overdrawn characters and overblown language work against a supposedly realistic narrative and create some incongruous effects.

The general recognition that his work is stylistically old-fashioned has contributed in some measure to the more extravagant criticisms of his skills as a novelist. It has also tended to obscure one of his most remarkable accomplishments in *Two Solitudes*: the self-reflexivity of his account of Paul Tallard's own "novel of Canada." The idea that the novel we have been reading is the novel that Paul has been working on before the outbreak of World War II not only sends us from the last words of *Two Solitudes* back to the first, but also makes a significant formal contribution to the unity the novel fails to establish in its thematic development.

For the most significant failings of *Two Solitudes* are more thematic than formal. MacLennan's "matter," far from being more important than his "manner," is deeply problematical on several counts, and this study has had occasion to suggest readings that challenge some of the most frequently expressed convictions of other commentators on the novel. It does not subscribe to the view that the marriage of Paul and Heather symbolizes the union of French and English Canada. Though impressed by MacLennan's depiction of ordinary French-Canadians, it does not on the whole find MacLennan's vaunted sympathies for French Canada very convincing. It does not find Paul a "weaker" character than Athanase Tallard. It raises other questions too, among them questions about how broad-minded Captain Yardley is and about why French-Canada is solely identified in Parts III and IV of the novel with a nationalist fanatic.

Many of these weaknesses in the novel are the weaknesses of the time in which it was written. Our view of what would constitute an acceptable reconciliation of the French and English of Canada has undergone vast changes in the period of nearly half a century since *Two Solitudes* was conceived. There is probably no idea of Canada greeted enthusiastically in 1945 that could please us today. It is therefore inevitable that a view of the novel that is heavily dependent on its content should result in a diminishment of MacLennan's reputation.

While proper attention must assuredly be paid to what MacLennan has to say about the French and the English, far more important in the long run will be our appreciation of the manner in which he has set about writing about the two solitudes together. The need to find a form to accommodate the fundamental dualism of the Canadian experience is after all as great today in 1990 as it was in 1945 — or in 1917.

Two Solitudes has been taken for granted for too long. We need to keep an eye on it, and every once in a while we need to reconsider it in the light of our own day. Times change and writing changes. There will always be more that needs to be said about MacLennan's novel, and if this re-reading stimulates others to re-read the novel for themselves it will have done what it set out to do.

NOTES

1. "I published at the height of the King era a book called *Two Solitudes* which sold more copies in Canada than any Canadian novel since *Maria Chapedelaine*. Literary merit had no connection with this sale; the book merely happened to put into words what hundreds of thousands of Canadians felt and knew" (Hugh MacLennan, *Scotchman's Return* 266); in the 6 February 1987 interview, Mac-Lennan said, "*Two Solitudes* . . . was the easiest book I ever wrote. It just came. It's not very well constructed, I don't think, and I'm not happy about the end of it."

2. The figure of 700,000 is quoted in Lucas, 5; the novel has subsequently sold a total of some 40,500 copies in Canada, nearly 15,000 of these since the Macmillan Paperback edition appeared in 1986. The source of these figures is Macmillan of Canada, December 1988.

3. Note dated 16 May 1966, appended to ms. of *Two Solitudes*, McGill University Rare Book Library.

4. See the letters from W.L. Graff to Hugh MacLennan, 7 July, 16 July, and 28 September 1944 (McGill University Rare Book Department) for a detailed discussion of Rilke's meaning.

5. For this translation see Michael Grant, *Roman Literature* (Harmondsworth, Eng.: Penguin, 1958), 9.

Works Cited

Alain, Albert. "Two Solitudes." *Le Devoir*, 28 avril 1945: 8.
    Highly critical review; comments on MacLennan's misleading depiction of French Canada.

Berand, Jean. "Le Roman 'Two Solitudes.' " *La Presse*, 14 avril 1945.
    Favourable review; comments on MacLennan's gift of sympathy for French Canada.

Boire, Gary. "Canadian (Tw)ink: Surviving the White-Outs." *Essays on Canadian Writing*, 35 (Winter 1987): 1–16.
    A discussion of colonialism is Canadian writing that comments on the neglect of Canada's indigenous people in *Two Solitudes*.

Bonenfant, Jean-Charles. "Les Livres canadiens-anglais." *La Revue de l'université Laval*, 4 avril 1950: 736–52.
    Includes a brief and informative account of *Two Solitudes*.

———. "Quatres romans recents." *La Revue de l'université Laval*, 6 September 1951: 51–54.
    Describes *Two Solitudes* as "typiquement Canadien" and expresses the hope that MacLennan's work will be translated into French.

Buitenhuis, Peter. *Hugh MacLennan*. Toronto: Forum House, 1969.
    A succinct (80-page) study of MacLennan's work to date. Buitenhuis draws effectively on comparisons between Canadian and American and British literary traditions; he considers *Two Solitudes*, especially in the earlier part, one of MacLennan's "most satisfying works."

Cameron, Elspeth. "Hugh MacLennan: An Annotated Bibliography." *The Annotated Bibliography of Canada's Major Authors*, ed. Robert Lecker and Jack David. 1. Downsview: ECW, 1979. 103–52.

———. *Hugh MacLennan: A Writer's Life*. Toronto: U of Toronto P, 1981.
    In this indispensable critical biography, Cameron has had access to MacLennan himself and to his various papers. In addition to chronicling his life, she comments on the fiction, viewing some of the flaws of *Two Solitudes* with a dispassionate eye and considering *Voices in Time* his greatest novel.

———, ed. *Hugh MacLennan: 1982*. Proceedings of the MacLennan Conference at University College, Toronto. Toronto: Canadian Studies Programme, University College, University of Toronto, 1982.

Includes valuable papers and responses to papers on the reception of MacLennnan's work in English and in French Canada as well as personal reminiscences by friends, colleagues, and other writers. Contributors include Antoine Sirois, W.J. Keith, Ben-Zion Shek, Marian Engel, Jacques Brazeau, Constance Beresford-Howe, and Solange Chaput-Rolland.

_____, ed. *The Other Side of Hugh MacLennan: Selected Essays Old and New.* Toronto: Macmillan, 1978.

Cockburn, Robert H. *The Novels of Hugh MacLennan.* Montreal: Harvest, 1971.

Cockburn is generally critical of MacLennan, considering he "has chosen to deliver his nationalistic campaign through the medium of fiction," but with various qualifications he considers the first half of *Two Solitudes* is skilfully and convincingly written."

Deacon, William Arthur. "French Canadian Problem in Daring and Timely Novel." *The Globe and Mail,* 7 April 1945: 18.

Two Solitudes is a social novel, and may be the best and most important Canadian novel ever published.

Denison, Merrill. "Where Two Civilizations Meet." *Saturday Review of Literature,* 10 Mar. 1945. Rpt. Goetsch, 1973, 101–04.

Favourable review by a historian. The novel "presents a sincere and unprejudiced picture of Canada's great internal conflict."

Fitzgerald, G.J. "Racial Problem." *The Gazette,* 31 Mar. 1945.

Two Solitudes "is the outstanding novel of this or any other year."

Goetsch, Paul, ed. *Hugh MacLennan.* Toronto: McGraw, 1973.

A useful collection of twenty articles and reviews of MacLennan's fiction. Includes work by George Woodcock, Hugo McPherson, Robert D. Chambers, William H. New, W.A. Deacon, Robertson Davies, and 1945 reviews of *Two Solitudes* by Merrill Denison and "I.M.S."

Heintzmann, Ralph, ed. *Journal of Canadian Studies* 14 (Winter 1979–80). [Special issue on Hugh MacLennan.]

Includes articles by Stephen Bonnycastle, Helen Hoy, and Francis Zichy.

"I.M.S." "Reviews of New Books." *Queen's Quarterly* 52 (Winter 1945): 494–96. Rpt. Goetsch, 1973, 97–99.

A sometimes scathing review.

Keefer, Janice K. *Under Eastern Eyes: A Critical Reading of Maritime Fiction.* Toronto: U of Toronto P, 1987.

MacLennan can be considered a regionalist on the understanding that his chosen region is not the Maritimes, but "that curious country, an Anglophone's Quebec." Interested in the Nova Scotian Captain Yardley.

Keith, W.J. *Canadian Literature in English.* London: Longman, 1985.

Considers MacLennan a didactic novelist and that "the marriage between

French-Canadian Paul and English-Canadian Heather . . . is a neat plot-conclusion that proves woefully inadequate at the level of socio-political ideas."

Kennedy, Leo. "Old and New Canada in a Major Novel." *Chicago Sun Book Week*, 21 Jan. 1945: 1.

Review describing *Two Solitudes* as the GREAT Canadian novel.

Lower, Arthur R.M. *Canadian Historical Review* 26 (1945): 326–28.

A favourable review by the eminent historian. *Two Solitudes* is "a milestone passed."

Lucas, Alec. *Hugh MacLennan*. Toronto: McClelland, 1970.

A brief (57-page), sympathetic, and idiosyncratic study that takes an unusually wide view of MacLennan's literary and historical context and draws on French-language commentary.

MacLennan, Hugh. *Barometer Rising*. New York: Duell, 1941.

_____ . *The Colour of Canada*. Toronto: McClelland, 1967.

_____ . *Cross-Country*. Toronto: Collins, 1949.

_____ . *Deux Solitudes*. Trans. Louise Gareau Des-Bois. Paris: Les Editions Spes, 1963.

_____ . *Each Man's Son*. Boston: Little, 1951.

_____ . *McGill: The Story of a University*. Ed. Hugh MacLennan. London: Allen, 1960.

_____ . *Oxyrhynchus: An Economic and Social Study*. [Doctoral Dissertation.] Princeton: Princeton UP, 1935.

_____ . *The Precipice*. New York: Duell, 1948.

_____ . *Return of the Sphinx*. New York: Scribner, 1967.

_____ . *Thirty and Three*. Ed. Dorothy Duncan. Toronto: Macmillan, 1954.

_____ . *Scotchman's Return and Other Essays*. Toronto: Macmillan, 1960.

_____ . *Seven Rivers of Canada*. New York: Scribner, 1961.

_____ . *Two Solitudes*. New York: Duell, 1945.

_____ . *Two Solitudes*. Toronto: Macmillan, 1951. Arranged by Claude T. Bissell.

_____ . *Two Solitudes*. Toronto: Macmillan, 1986.

_____ . *The Watch That Ends the Night*. New York: Scribner, 1959.

_____ . *Voices in Time*. Toronto: Macmillan, 1980.

MacLulich, T.D. *Hugh MacLennan*. Boston: Twayne, 1983.

This is the only study of all MacLennan's published work. MacLulich considers MacLennan's books "are cut from the same Tory cloth as the history of Donald Creighton and the philosophy of George Grant," and he argues that MacLennan's writing has been shaped as much by private emotional imperatives as by reasoned responses to external political and social conditions.

Maheux, Abbé Arthur. "A Masterpiece: Un Chef d'oeuvre." *Montreal Star*, 15 Sept. 1945.

Favourable bilingual review commenting on MacLennan's success in solving national problems.

Mathews, Robin. *Canadian Literature: Surrender or Revolution.* Toronto: Steel Rail, 1978.

Devotes a chapter, "Hugh MacLennan: The Nationalist Dilemma," to a discussion of MacLennan as an anti-colonialist and anti-imperialist.

McNaught, Eleanor. Rev. of *Two Solitudes. The Canadian Forum,* May 1945: 46.

Favourable review. Considers *Two Solitudes* reflects the substance of Canada and marks a new maturity in the Canadian novel.

McPherson, Hugo. "Fiction 1940–1960." *Literary History of Canada: Canadian Literature in English.* Ed. Carl F. Klinck, *et al.* Toronto: U of Toronto P, 1965: 694–723.

A witty account of MacLennan's early novels in a broadly social and historical context. The claim for MacLennan's centrality to Canadian literature, McPherson says, has not been effectively challenged.

Metcalf, John. *What Is a Canadian Literature?* Guelph, Ont.: Red Kite, 1988.

A wideranging criticism of Canadian literary criticism.

Morley, Patricia. *The Immoral Moralists: Hugh MacLennan and Leonard Cohen.* Toronto: Clarke, 1972.

In this discussion of puritanism in the work of MacLennan and of Cohen, Morley argues that the heroic characters in *Two Solitudes* challenge the puritan values dominant in both French and English Canada.

Pelletier, Claude, comp. *Écrivains canadiens-anglais: dossiers de presse.* Sherbrooke, QC: Bibliothèque du seminaire de Sherbrooke, 1986.

Reviews and articles about MacLennan from French- and English-language publications.

Prescott, Orville. "Books of the Times." *The New York Times,* 17 Jan. 1945.

A very favourable review. The novel is "superbly vital."

Shek, Ben-Zion. "Commentary on Antoine Sirois," in Cameron, ed. *Hugh MacLennan: 1982,* 123–31.

Discusses the delay in publishing a French translation of *Two Solitudes* and considers the influence of French-Canadian criticisms of *Two Solitudes,* particularly those of Jean Ethier-Blais.

Stevenson, Warren. "A Neglected Theme in *Two Solitudes." Canadian Literature* 75 (Winter 1977): 53–60.

Focussed principally of the theme of individual self-awareness in the novel, this is the only essay to discuss the "ultimate solitude."

Stratford, Philip. *All the Polarities: Comparative Studies in Contemporary Canadian Novels in French and English.* Toronto: ECW, 1986.

One chapter is in large part devoted to *Two Solitudes.* Stratford is critical of the love scene between Paul and Heather, and describes MacLennan as "shouldering in to give historical depth to the narrative."

Symons, Scott. *Place d'Armes.* Toronto: McClelland, 1967.

An experimental novel set in Montreal during the 1960s.

Trilling, Diana. "Fiction in Review." *The Nation* 24 Feb. 1945: 227–28.
Critical review. Considers this is one of those rare instances in which an author's seriousness and decency do a very good job as proxy for art.

University of Calgary Libraries, Special Collections. *The Hugh MacLennan Papers: An Inventory of the Archive at the University of Calgary Libraries.* Calgary: U of Calgary P, 1986.

Wade, Mason. "Almost the Great Canadian Novel; The Best Yet Written." *Canadian Register,* 28 Apr. 1945, qtd. in Cameron 1981, 185.

Wilson, Edmund. *O Canada: An American's Notes on Canadian Culture.* New York: Farrar, 1964.
Wilson feels that in his earnest and ambitious attempt to cover his large self-assignment MacLennan sometimes embarks upon themes which he believes to be socially important but which do not really excite his imagination.

Woodcock, George. *Hugh MacLennan.* Toronto: Copp, 1969.
Considers that MacLennan, "an unashamedly didactic writer," occupies a position "of uneasy eminence in Canadian letters." The conclusion of *Two Solitudes* is "contrived to fit a nationalist message."

Unpublished manuscripts, original typescripts of published novels, correspondence, and other archival materials are collected in the Hugh MacLennan Papers, Department of Rare Books and Special Collections, McGill University, Montreal, and in the Hugh MacLennan Papers at the University of Calgary Libraries. Other archival materials are among the MacLennan Papers at the McCord Museum in Montreal; in the Macmillan Archive at McMaster University, Hamilton; in the Thomas Fisher Rare Book Library at the University of Toronto; and in the National Archives of Canada.

Index